THE NEW MIDDLEWOMEN
Profitable Banking Through
On-Lending Groups

THE NEW MIDDLEWOMEN

PROFITABLE BANKING THROUGH
ON-LENDING GROUPS

*Malcolm Harper, Ezekiel Esipisu,
A.K. Mohanty and D.S.K. Rao*

INTERMEDIATE TECHNOLOGY PUBLICATIONS 1998

Intermediate Technology Publications Ltd.
103–105 Southampton Row, London WCIB 4HH, UK

© 1998, Malcolm Harper *et. al.*

A CIP catalogue record for this book is available from the British Library

ISBN 1 85339 431 9

Printed in India

ACKNOWLEDGEMENTS

The four co-authors who are named on the cover would like to make it clear that they were no more than the coordinators and leaders of the study teams. They would like particularly to acknowledge the work of the following colleagues, whose names would also have appeared as co-authors were there space to print them:

Bankers Institute of Rural Development (BIRD): P. Satish, Girija Srinivasan, Dushyant S Chauhan, H.S. Subramayana, (consultant).

Kenya Rural Enterprise Programme (K-Rep): Marceline Obuya.

Centre for Development Research and Training, Xavier Institute of Management (CENDERET/XIM): Gilbert Ravichander, Babita Mahapatra and Satya N Mohanty.

Space does not allow us to list the names of other colleagues who helped so much, but their collaboration is nonetheless gratefully acknowledged.

We must also place on record our sincere gratitude to the Directors of Cranfield School of Management, BIRD, K-Rep and CENDERET/XIM, for their encouragement. The study was funded by the Economic and Social Research Management Unit (ESRMU) of the Department for International Development (DFID) of the British Government, and the New Delhi office of the Ford Foundation. We thank them for their support, and we hope that their investment in this study will earn a good return in improved financial services to poorer people and thus to the alleviation of poverty.

Above all, however, we thank the women and the men who are actually involved in On-Lending Groups, the group members and the staff of the many banks and non-government organisations, in India, Kenya and elsewhere, who so generously answered our questions and shared their experience with us. We were encouraged and inspired by their enthusiasm and commitment to working with groups, and we hope that their example, as described in this book, will encourage others to emulate them.

We are all too aware that people who make a living from micro-enterprises, unlike academics, or even bankers and NGO staff, only earn when they are working. Time spent answering questions is time not spent doing business. We hope this book will bring more financial institutions into the field, and the group members from whom we learned so much, and the many millions like them who need financial services, will eventually benefit from the greater competition that should result.

LIST OF ABBREVIATIONS

AKAY	Amalar Kutumba Abhivriddhi Yojana
AKRSP	Aga Khan Rural Support Programme
BBK	Barclays Bank of Kenya
BIRD	Bankers Institute of Rural Development
BRAC	Bangladesh Rural Advancement Committee
BRI	Bank Rakyat Indonesia
CENDERET	Centre for Development Research and Training
CO	Credit Officers (K-Rep)
DANIDA	Danish International Development Agency
DFID	Department for International Development
FFH	Freedom from Hunger
GEMINI	Growth and Equity through Micro-enterprise Investment
GMVM	Gramin Mahila va Balak Vikas Mandal
IYD	Institute of Youth Development
K-Rep	Kenya Rural Enterprise Programme
KCB	Kenya Commercial Bank
KEPP	Kenya Enterprise Promotion Programme
Ksh	Kenya Shilling (converted to US$ @ $1.00=Ksh. 55)
KWFT	Kenya Women's Finance Trust
MYRADA	Mysore Resettlement and Development Agency
NABARD	National Bank for Agriculture and Rural Development
NGO	Non-Government Organisation
NPSS	New Public School Samiti
PHBK	Proyek Pengembangan Hubugan Bank KSM
PRADAN	Professional Assistance for Development Action
ROSCA	Rotating Savings and Credit Association
RRB	Regional Rural Bank
Rs.	India Rupee (converted to US$ @ $1.00=Rs. 35)
SANASA	Federation of Thrift and Credit Cooperative Societies
SEWA	Self-Employed Women's Association
SHG	Self-Help Group
SIDBI	Small Industries Development Bank of India
SOPORTE	Society for Promotion of Rural Technology and Education

TRDEP	Thana Resource Development and Advancement Programme
UP	Uttar Pradesh
XIM	Xavier Institute of Management
YCO	Youth Charitable Organisation

CONTENTS

CHAPTER 1

INTRODUCTION

1.1. What are On-Lending Groups?

Middlemen and moneylenders are often portrayed as the twin villains and exploiters of the poor. This book is about a new kind of middlemen, or more often middlewomen, who are also moneylenders. These women have shown that their groups can develop into effective links, or intermediaries, between commercial banks and the poor, to the mutual benefit of both.

These groups have almost as many names as there are languages. The most common English name for the traditional groups from which this type of activity has emerged is "Rotating Savings and Credit Association" or ROSCA. In India they are usually called Self-Help Groups (SHGs). The term self-help has very individualist connotations, and was coined by Samuel Smiles in his book of that title in 1859, to describe people whom we might today call entrepreneurs; the critical factor that he identified in their success, however, was not their individualism but their willingness to help themselves rather than waiting for others to help them. That is exactly what the groups here do, but in the process they can also help banks to reach a new and profitable market.

The term 'On-Lending Groups' has been chosen for the groups described here. This term is less familiar than 'solidarity groups' or 'self-help groups', but it is used by some agencies which deal with several different types of groups, in order to distinguish their particular functions. We use it because it clearly singles out the particular intermediation functions which they perform. We hesitate to coin yet another specialist term in a field where there are already far too many, but we hope that it will clarify the particular features of the groups discussed here.

These On-Lending Groups are similar in many respects to the groups which are the foundation of the success of the Grameen Bank in Bangladesh and the many similar programmes throughout the world, but they are very different in one critical way. The Grameen Bank type of group, and the solidarity groups which are part of similar programmes in Latin America, act as collectors of savings and repayment, as loan appraisers, and above all as guarantors, but the groups themselves do not borrow and do not lend. They facilitate and indeed make possible the operations of the bank or other financial agency, but they do not act as a bank themselves.

Our On-Lending Groups, however, are actually micro-banks. They collect their own equity capital, and savings deposits, from their owners, who are also the members and the customers, they lend out their money to their members, at interest rates which they decide, and they accumulate profits which they choose either to distribute to the owners, or to add to the fund at their joint disposal.

A great deal has been written about the solidarity or Grameen Bank type of group, which is the basis of most of the best-known "new generation" of microfinance institutions, and it is often not clear that the loans are not to the groups but to the members individually. Barenbach and Guzman (1994, p. 122), for instance, in their survey of worldwide solidarity group experience, state that the "sum of each loan is lent to the group as a whole"; this does not mean, however, that the group actually borrows and re-lends; the loans are indeed guaranteed by the group, but they are lent to and repaid by the individual members.

These systems avoid many of the high transaction costs which are normally associated with direct loans to small borrowers, or direct collection of savings, but the bank still has to maintain individual records for each customer, and has to be familiar with, if not directly to control, the ways in which each borrower uses his, or more likely her, money, and their individual repayment records.

If a bank accepts savings from an On-Lending Group, or lends money to it, the banker need not know the details of the individual members, or their uses of the money, any more than a depositor in a bank needs to know who is borrowing the money he has deposited, or how it is being used. So long as he is confident of the management of the bank itself, its ability to select good borrowers who will make good use of his money, and will let him have it back, with interest, he needs to know no more.

The relationship between a bank and an On-Lending Group is in fact similar to that of a manufacturer of toothpaste and the small retail outlets through which the product reaches the public. The manufacturer is interested in the final consumers from the point of view of market research, but he is not concerned with the details of every retail sale of the toothpaste. The shopkeeper receives a margin on the selling price which pays him for the distribution service he provides, and it would be totally uneconomical for the manufacturer to concern himself with each sale. The manufacturer chooses to distribute his goods through independent shopkeepers because it is more effective, and less expensive, than operating his own retail outlets. In the same way, banks can use On-Lending Groups to reach more customers, more efficiently.

The Village Bank system which has been promoted by some organisations is more similar to On-Lending Groups than are the Grameen Bank type solidarity groups, but Village Banks are usually initiated by an outside NGO and their initial capital consists of a loan or grant from this organisation, not members' savings. Their members are also bound by the regulations of the sponsoring NGO, with rigid loan cycles and so on; they are not free to manage their own bank in the way that members of a On-Lending Group are.

It is perhaps understandable that the terminology is not clear. The whole micro-finance movement, or industry as it has now become, is very new. Our

On-Lending Groups are solidarity groups, in the sense of being solid and sharing common goals, and they are in fact independent village banks in a very real way. The names are unimportant; what matters is that the different systems are clearly recognised for what they are, regardless of the titles by which they are known.

The growth rates, the repayment records and the positive social impact of the solidarity or Grameen bank type institutions are impressive, and there is little question that the many new institutions which are building systems of that type will continue to expand and to multiply. Some of the larger institutions have also been able to raise debt finance at market rates on national capital markets, albeit often with government or other guarantees. They are still however, dependent on subsidy or "social investors" for their initial equity capital, and there appear to be few if any cases where profit-seeking private investors have put their money into microfinance institutions of this sort.

Large sums have been committed to the cause of microfinance, at the microcredit summit and on other occasions, but it is at least arguable that genuine large-scale expansion of microfinance will not take place if it depends on grants, subsidised loans or any other type of non-commercial assistance. Successful mass-marketing depends on a good product and on a distribution chain in which every link is profitable. Small short-term loans and flexible savings instruments have been shown to be good products, for which their customers are willing to pay a price which can support effective distribution. When commercial banks use On-Lending Groups as the final link in their distribution chain, every party can be satisfied.

The repayment records of most microfinance institutions show quite clearly that poor people, who save and borrow small amounts of money, are bankable. Bankability, however, is not the same as profitability, and as Remenyi puts it (1993, p.129), the aim here is to demonstrate "to the hard-headed that the poor are a much-neglected investment opportunity". On-Lending Groups are a distribution channel through which the new market can profitably be reached, not just by new institutions which have been set up for the purpose but by any commercial bank which has branches within reasonable reach of these new customers.

There are a number of ways in which this new channel can be used. The Foundation for Development Cooperation (1992), in one of the few publications which have focused specifically on On-Lending Groups, identified three different routes through which banks do business with these groups, and through them with their members.

- Direct from the lender to the On-Lending Group, with no facilitating intermediary, which is usual in Kenya and becoming more common in India.
- Direct from the bank to the On-Lending Group with facilitation from a NGO, which is the most common route in India.
- From the bank to a microfinance NGO which on-lends to, and collects deposits from, the On-Lending Group; this is common in Indonesia, the Philippines, Sri Lanka and India.

The aim is to study a number of these banking relationships in some detail, in order to show that On-Lending Groups can be profitable customers.

1.2. Are On-Leading Groups a Market for Existing Banks?

The history of business is replete with examples of long-established institutions which have failed to recognise new markets. The railways and the shipping lines had finance and existing customers, and they understood the travel market. They should surely have recognised the new opportunities offered by air travel. Nevertheless, the airline business had to be developed by new, independent entrepreneurs who appeared to lack everything the older companies had, but did have the vision to recognise the new opportunity. The large mainframe computer companies failed to recognise the need for smaller personal and portable computers, and the market for mobile phones was developed by new entrants into the communications business, rather than by the traditional telephone operating companies.

The record thus far suggests that the microfinance market may be yet another example of a lost opportunity. There is, however, one important difference which makes it all the more important, and more possible, for existing banks to grasp the potential which this market offers, and to work through On-Lending Groups to reach it. The 'brave new world' (Otero and Rhyne, 1994) of microfinance is not only a world of new institutions, it is a world which is built on a foundation of subsidy and foreign aid. The new institutions are beginning to access savings and capital markets on a commercial basis, but the pace of expansion is dependent more on pledges of international assistance than on profit-seeking investors.

The commercial banks are not therefore, like the railway companies or the mainframe computer manufacturers, in the position of trying to catch up with successful profitable businesses which have taken the initiative from them. The competition, if it can be called that, still consists of no more than some 7000 institutions, which in July 1997 were said to be reaching about eight million people (Grameen Trust, 1997). The majority of the institutions are very small, reaching only a few hundred customers, and although the total achievement is remarkable, only a minute proportion of the total market has thus far been reached.

It could be argued, in fact, that the subsidies have achieved their objective, in that they have shown that the poor are good customers, and have supported a wide range of experiments with different marketing channels. The time is now ripe for established commercial banks, which have the necessary physical, financial and human resources, to enter the market which has thus been 'discovered'. On-Lending Groups offer a channel through which they can do this without having to set up special units, departments or subsidiaries, since they can be treated like any other savings or loan customer.

The declaration which emerged from the widely publicised microcredit summit suggests that microfinance is all about new institutions. The local commercial banks may have a role to provide savings and loan facilities to 'the microenterprise program as a client' (Microcredit Summit, 1996, p.21), but "when growth has gone beyond the capacity of local banks" there is said to be a need for new institutions or special operations. There will be a need for "special microfinance departments and subinstitutions" (ibid., p.23). One of the particular merits of On-Lending Groups is that they do not need special treatment, and can therefore be part of the client portfolio of any branch bank.

The extensive literature on microfinance has generally neglected On-Lending Groups, partly because their role in the industry has thus far been quite limited, and perhaps because new institutions, with totally new systems, are more exciting than a new marketing channel for existing institutions. The new channel has itself evolved from one of the oldest forms of human association, which perhaps makes it even less newsworthy. The microfinance industry has also thus far been driven by donors and other providers of subsidised support, rather than by the market. An approach which is unlikely to need long-term subsidy, and institutions which owe nothing to donors, may be less attractive to those whose own livelihood depends on the continuation of non-commercial assistance.

Remenyi (1993, p. 55, table 2.1) suggests a typology of methods of microfinance, with three groups and three models within each group, but his types do not properly include the model whereby banks do business direct with On-Lending Groups. His solidarity groups are small facilitating groups of five or six members, on the Grameen Bank model, and the only equivalent to our approach is the traditional credit cooperative model, which is sadly but rightly dismissed as being mainly for the less poor.

Remenyi's ROSCA model does not include the possibility of direct financial linkages between the groups and formal institutions. Direct links are only included in his 'broker' model which is for individuals rather than groups. He states (p.117) that the broker model has not facilitated the independent flow of bank finance to the poor, but has rather enabled banks to avoid facing the issue of how they themselves can interface directly with the poor.

Bankers should not try to deal directly with the poor, just as the manufacturer of toothpaste does not deal directly with every customer. The banker may set up a special unit, as is suggested in the microcredit summit declaration. This is difficult and expensive. The most successful example, the Village Unit system of the Bank Rakhyat Indonesia, was set up to make use of an existing network of branches when the heavily subsidised programme for which they had been established was wound up. Had this network not already existed, it is probable that the village unit system would never have been developed.

Alternatively, the bank may look for intermediaries. Many shopkeepers, traders and moneylenders already play this role. They obtain credit from the banks, or from suppliers who borrow from banks, and they then extend credit to their poorer customers who themselves cannot borrow directly from a bank. This form of indirect finance is universal, and can be both equitable and efficient if there is adequate competition, if customers are well informed, and if credit is available for a wide choice of commodities. These conditions, however, are by no means always satisfied, particularly when the eventual customers have little purchasing power.

One of the many reasons for the relative failure of most government-sponsored poverty-alleviation loan programmes is that the banks are compelled to deal directly with very small clients, rather than working through intermediaries. These clients are not a viable customer group for direct business, and it is almost inevitable that other "informal" intermediaries will become involved as brokers, sponsors or facilitators, even if they do not actually take title to the money. Local bureaucrats, politicians or the bank staff themselves perform the bridging function, for a consideration, and the end result is that the clients are little better-off than before.

The GEMINI set of issues papers (1995) on micro-enterprise development, which is in some sense a survey of the "state of the art" of the whole field, including microfinance, also fails to cover On-Lending Groups. As in Remenyi's typology, and most of the other literature, facilitating solidarity groups are included, but not On-Lending Groups which are genuine microbanks in their own right.

1.3. Why should the Banks Bother with On-lending Groups?

Foreign donors and national governments are rightly willing to devote resources to microfinance because it can help to reduce poverty. Bankers are presumably as concerned as anyone else about poverty, because they feel for their fellow-men and also because in a general sense their banks will be more profitable if society as a whole is more prosperous. If, however, microfinance services are ever to be 'massified', and to become as available to all those who need them as any other mass market consumer product or service, bankers will have to be motivated by something stronger than social concern or general enthusiasm for prosperity.

Described in this text in some detail are a number of examples of successful and profitable linkages between On-Lending Groups and banks, in India and in Kenya. There are also many other similar examples, in other countries, which are equally convincing. The Bank Shinta Daya, a private bank in Indonesia, attempted to reach smaller clients by working through an NGO, but failed either to reach the intended customers or to cover its costs (Bank Poor, 1996, p.10). The Bank then hired its own field staff to identify and work with On-Lending Groups as intermediaries. The venture was highly successful, and these groups now make up 29% of the borrowers and 85% of the savers on the Bank's books. The benefits of the savings service, to both parties, were as great as those of the advances.

Bankers are naturally and rightly, conservative, which makes them slow to enter any new field. Donor enthusiasm, and the results of the best-known institutions in Bangladesh and elsewhere, may also have created the impression that microfinance can never be genuinely profitable. Nevertheless, a number of commercial banks are already doing business with On-Lending Groups, albeit usually on a small scale. The Habib Bank has a number of accounts with such groups in Karachi, Hatton National Bank is working with them in Sri Lanka, and the Rastriya Banija Bank and the Bank of the Philippine Islands have also entered this market in Nepal and the Philippines (Foundation for Development Cooperation, 1992, pp. 31-32).

A number of commercial banks are also lending to microfinance projects and institutions, in East Africa, in the northeastern United States and Canada, and elsewhere, but these loans are usually at concessional rates. The accounts are regarded as investments in social responsibility or public relations, rather than as mainstream business. Examined later in more detail, is what stops banks from going into the On-Lending Group market with more enthusiasm, and that there are a number of reasons why they should look at it more seriously.

First and foremost, doing business with On-Lending Groups can be profitable in its own right, so it need not be justified as a "loss leader" whose losses will be covered by profits from other activities. Readers will be able to judge its profitability for themselves, from the detailed data which follows, but there are also other arguments in its favour in addition to its intrinsic profitability.

Today's members of On-Lending Groups are tomorrow's individual customers, for savings and borrowing products, and successful business people are likely to be loyal to the first financial institution with which they did business. One of the main reasons why many NGOs and other "new generation" microfinance institutions are aiming to become full-fledged banks is that even their long-standing microfinance clients, who now need and are able to manage individual services, are unwilling to "graduate" to "real" banks, even if they are encouraged and assisted to do so.

They believe that banks are not for "ordinary" people like themselves, and their previous experience may have given them good cause for this belief. The millions of customers who are already being served by the new institutions may be lost for ever to the banks. The numbers are small now, but growing, and if banks wish to retain their market share they should be trying to be the "first" bank for more people than the few new customers who enter their branches directly.

Table 1 summarises the scale of On-Lending Group financing in Kenya by five of the main institutions, in mid-1997.

Table 1. On-Lending Group Financing in Kenya, 1997

MFIs	K-Rep	KWFT	Faulu	Care Kenya	Danida	Total
Year started	1990	1992	1992	1989	1996	–
Number of On-Lending Groups	778	238	152	652	12	1832
Number of members	12,718	4760	3612	13000	360	34,450
Amount lent (in $ millions)	21.2 mn.	3.46 mn	4.25 mn	0.98 mn.	0.33 mn.	29.9 mn
Recovery rate (%)	98	97	99	95	80	–

The commercial banks have played virtually no part in this quite substantial activity, apart from providing "social responsibility" funds to some of the institutions at heavily subsidised rates of interest. Some thirty million dollars of loans have been disbursed, at rates of interest which are generally well over the rates charged by the banks, and one would have thought that business of this scale would have attracted attention on commercial, as opposed to welfare grounds.

In India itself, from which much of the detailed evidence is drawn, there are generous incentives to encourage commercial banks to do business with On-Lending Groups. In Orissa, one of the States where this study was conducted, the programme to promote bank "linkages" with groups has been vigorously and consistently pursued, and there are large numbers of NGOs working in rural areas. The

State is in fact regarded as one of the leaders in this new area of bank activity. Orissa has around one-third more people than the whole of Kenya, so that one might have expected substantially larger numbers of groups to have had access to institutional finance there; the figures given in Table 2 show that this has not been the case.

Table 2: Orissa, On-Lending Groups Borrowing from Banks

Year	Number of groups	Amount lent	Number of bank branches
1994 / 95	383	$ 58,000	8
1995 / 96	103	$ 24,000	17
1996 / 97	292	$ 58,000	31

As a result of this reluctance, in Orissa and the rest of India, many other new organisations are entering the market. The Small Industries Development Bank of India (SIDBI) in three years financed 75 NGOs, which had little previous experience in banking operations, to on-lend around Rs. 100 million, or almost three million dollars, to about 10,000 On-Lending Groups, with about 200,000 members. This volume of business is similar to that which has been achieved by all the commercial banks in the country in some seven years, in spite of the fact that the banks charge 12% interest, as opposed to the 15% charged by the NGOs. This shows very clearly that On-Lending Groups need funds, and are able to pay for them.

On-Lending Groups are also a uniquely effective way of reaching one particular market which banks worldwide have neglected, in spite of the fact that it constitutes around half the population, everywhere, that is, women. The social and economic status of women is changing even in the most conservative countries, and women are becoming more active as business owners, heads of households and financial decision makers. Men also participate in these groups, but less commonly than women, and one of the most effective ways in which a bank could increase its proportion of women customers would be to start doing business with On-Lending Groups.

Established commercial banks are facing competition on another front. Large-scale corporate business was traditionally profitable, and these clients tended to be loyal to their existing banking connections. Financial liberalisation means that national banks have to compete with international institutions, which operate on a global basis, and which are not burdened by large local branch networks. New local banks and other financial institutions are also coming up, which specialise in particular functions, or which have close personal connections with large businesses.

The banks must compete in these markets, but they should also take advantage of their one major strength, their large branch networks. The Managing Director of Bank Pertanian, Malaysia's successful rural development bank, believes that the future will lie in the "rediscovery of retail banking" (NABARD-APRACA 1996, p.111). Small retail branches may in the past have been a liability in some countries, since so much of their business was tied up in unprofitable government-sponsored schemes, but On-Lending Groups offer one profitable market segment which is ideal for branches which are located in less prosperous areas. It is not suggested that a branch can sustain itself solely on On-Lending Group business, but it can make up a significant and profitable share of a branch's portfolio.

What is fundamentally needed is a change of attitude; bankers must learn to regard poor people not as objects of charity but 'as an additional opportunity for investment with profit' (Magill, 1994, p.79). Financial services for this market should be seen not as 'a handmaiden of non-financial objectives such as poverty alleviation, social cooperation or the empowerment of women' (Rutherford, 1995), but as worthwhile banking business in its own right. In this way, banks will profitably expand their customer base, and in the process they will help the poor people to be less poor.

One authoritative group recommended that NGOs should encourage On-Lending Groups to do business with banks in places where NGOs themselves were unlikely to be allowed to become legal financial entities (Bank Poor, 1996). It is surely paradoxical that banks should be regarded as the last resort, when they should be the obvious first choice as a source of financial services.

1.4. The Scope and Methodology of the Study

This study was undertaken in order to obtain answers to a number of questions about the financial and social aspects of intermediation through On-Lending Groups. There is already a certain amount of published material on the subject, notably that originating from or encouraged by the Foundation for Development Cooperation of Brisbane, Australia. The National Bank for Agriculture and Rural Development (NABARD) in India has also sponsored and published a number of studies on On-Lending Groups. It appears fairly well understood, for instance, that the majority of members do benefit as a result of their membership, in social as well as economic terms, and that they can afford to pay the apparently high rates of interest which many of the groups voluntarily impose on themselves.

There are, however, a number of other important issues where there is less evidence, and less certainty. Some are "social", in that they relate to the degree to which On-Lending Group membership contributes to poverty alleviation, and others are about the cost and feasibility of using these groups as financial intermediaries.

The questions which we attempted to address are listed here:

About the groups and their members:

- Are there large numbers of potential groups in most communities, already involved in some sort of cash or in-kind saving and lending, and if there are, how easy is it for them to evolve into suitable banking intermediaries?
- Are the poor (meaning the poorest who can benefit from loans, and repay without hardship) members of such groups?
- Can a group function with no literate members and no routine outside help, or must an NGO person or other literate outsider always act as manager or secretary?

- Do the loans and their repayment genuinely really benefit all members, so that they are better-off than before ?
- What proportion of members default or drop out, and are they as a result worse-off than before ?

About the use of groups for financial intermediation:

- Does outside money 'spoil' the groups, reduce their motivation, or demand too much of their management ?
- How can On-Lending Groups be developed most effectively and brought to the required level for borrowing from banks? How long does this process take?
- How can groups be assessed most efficiently, what objective and other indicators can be used to judge that a group is a good intermediary ?
- What is the cost of the group development and assessment tasks? Are these tasks most efficiently undertaken by a bank or by an NGO ?
- Can On-Lending Groups afford to pay interest rates which are high enough for their business to be profitable for the banks which lend to them ?
- How can a group's own savings be used as security in ways which members will take seriously but which does not mean that they are effectively borrowing their own money ?
- What really stops banks from lending to On-Lending Groups ? Is it ignorance, on which side, is it because groups do not approach banks, because groups do not need loans from banks, because groups lack security or are not registered legal bodies or because assessing groups takes too long or is too difficult ?
- Will groups eventually build their own funds and no longer need outside money, or will their needs grow with their access, so they continue to borrow from the bank?

It would have been possible to search for the answers to these questions in many different countries, and it is of course impossible to generalise; evidence from one place might lead to quite different conclusions than from elsewhere. This study, however, was carried out in India and Kenya.

The choice of India is obvious. India has the highest number of people in poverty, and poor people are the main beneficiaries of membership of these groups, and are thus the main market. There has also been a more concerted effort in India than anywhere else to promote financial links between On-Lending Groups and commercial banks. Numbers of banks have been involved, and they have worked direct with the groups as well as through a wide variety of NGOs. This national effort has also been heavily subsidised, so that it is difficult to draw conclusions as to the genuine economics of the groups themselves, and of the banks' linkages with them, but the subsidies are fairly transparent, so hopefully they have not concealed the financial realities.

India has almost one-fifth of the world's population, and there is more diversity within India than between many radically different countries. The study was carried out in four States, Uttar Pradesh in the northern heartland, Orissa in the generally poorer eastern part of the country, Karnataka in the rather more progressive south, with its longer tradition of informal savings and credit groups, and Maharashtra in the west. Uttar Pradesh on its own would be the world's fifth most populous country, and the other States are individually all far larger than Kenya or many other independent nations. The choice of groups, banks and NGOs within these States was determined by convenience, existing contacts and the existence of particular types of group/bank relationships.

In Kenya virtually no commercial banks have lent money to On-Lending Groups, and it may therefore appear to be a strange choice. However, a number of NGOs have financial relationships with these groups in Kenya. Some of these NGOs are specialised only in microfinance, and they are working towards becoming independent financial institutions. The Kenya Rural Enterprise Programme (K-Rep), the market leader in this nascent industry, is about to acquire the legal status of a bank, and has for some years been operating like one. Its experience is therefore highly relevant to our study.

The detailed field work was carried out by three different institutions, each of which is working with On-Lending Groups and the agencies which promote and finance them, albeit in very different ways. Each of these was asked to address the above questions, but they were also interested to use this study to inform and improve their own work in this field. Because each had its own agenda, they obtained and analysed the information in a variety of different ways which are not always consistent or directly comparable with one another. This book attempts to consolidate their findings.

The Centre for Development Research and Training (CENDERET) at the Xavier Institute of Management (XIM) in Bhubaneswar, Orissa, is unusual in that it is devoted to poverty alleviation in Orissa, one of India's poorest states, but is at the same time an integral part of one of India's more prestigious post-graduate management schools, which offers a two year MBA type programme for young men and women whose main interest is to obtain jobs in the corporate sector. The relationship is not always easy, but each benefits from the other.

CENDERET works mainly through an extensive network of NGOs which it has developed in Orissa. It offers training, consultancy and institutional support to them and to Indian and international institutions, and also itself manages a range of projects in fields such as primary education, enterprise development, social forestry and watershed management. Many of the NGOs with which CENDERET works have promoted On-Lending Groups, or Self-Help Groups as they are called in India; some of them are themselves financing them with funds they have obtained from Indian development institutions or foreign donors, and other have linked the groups to commercial banks. CENDERET has also been contracted by NABARD to offer a series of short exposure programmes on On-Lending Group linkage to bankers and NGOs from Orissa, West Bengal and the northeastern states, and the results of this study will be used in these programmes.

The Bankers Institute for Rural Development (BIRD), Lucknow, was established by NABARD to provide training and research for all the many institutions which are involved in rural finance in India. It is now an autonomous institution, and offers a wide range of training programmes for senior staff and branch management of the commercial and regional rural banks, and for staff from the cooperative banking sector. It also provides training and material for trainers who themselves train rural banking staff. BIRD has also organised international training on behalf of a number of international agencies.

BIRD's staff have undertaken a number of studies of On-Lending Groups, and this study builds on and is reinforced by this experience. Its results will be used in BIRD's training, and will also inform the policy advice which BIRD is frequently asked to provide through NABARD to the Reserve Bank and the Government of India.

K-Rep is one of the best known microfinance institutions in Africa, and is indeed well known internationally. Unlike CENDERET and BIRD, K-Rep is actually directly involved in financing On-Lending Groups itself, and will shortly be operating as a bank. K-Rep might therefore be considered an inappropriate choice to carry out a dispassionate study into selected social and financial aspects of On-Lending Group intermediation. The research and consultancy department of K-Rep has however been clearly separated from the banking function, in preparation for when the bank will be separately incorporated as such, and the remaining sections will be left to continue their non-banking functions. This department of K-Rep has already carried out a number of assignments for international agencies and microfinance institutions in Kenya, other countries in Africa and elsewhere, offering training, consultancy and management services. The results of this study are expected substantially to enhance the knowledge base of this work, as well as being of immediate value to K-Rep's banking operations in Kenya itself.

Table 3 summarises the number of On-Lending Groups and their members, and the banks and NGOs which worked with them, which were studied by the respective institutions.

Table 3. The Samples in India and Kenya

	Groups	Members		NGOs	Banks	Branches
		Women	Men			
CENDERET	20	281	75	16	12	13
BIRD	52	701	195	31	11	18
K-Rep	16	173	87	N/A	N/A	N/A
Total	88	1155	357	47	33	31

All three institutions also interviewed staff of a number of other relevant institutions. K-Rep in particular interviewed representatives of all the other major microfinance NGOs in Kenya, as well as senior and branch level staff of the main commercial banks.

The actual study was carried out using a combination of individual structured and unstructured interviews with group members and officers, and with concerned staff of the other institutions, together with several focus group discussions with larger numbers of members.

The chapters and subsections which follow are structured around these questions. Some evidence is presented from published material and other sources about On-Lending Groups. This is followed by the findings from the four states in India and from Kenya. Each sub-section ends with a very short case study illustrating the issue which is being addressed, and with a summary of the answer to the question. The text is concluded with a review of the conclusions, and some suggestions and recommendations.

CHAPTER 2

THE GROUPS AND THEIR DEVELOPMENT

2.1. Do Groups Already Exist ?

Rotating Savings and Credit Associations, or ROSCAs, are the original from which our On-Lending Groups have evolved. Ardener's definition (Ardener and Burman, 1995, p.1) is clear:

"an association formed upon a core of participants who make regular contributions to a fund which is given in whole or in part to each contributor in turn".

The contribution may be either in money, or in kind. Grain funds are common among subsistence farmers everywhere, and groups may contribute stones for house building, their own labour or almost any other commodity which people can provide individually in small quantities but which becomes much more useful when it is available in a large amount.

Because they are known by so many different names, and they can operate in such a variety of ways, these groups are often not recognised for what they are. Many readers of this book, for instance, particularly women, probably make regular contributions of some sort towards a common fund, but because it is embedded in some other social activity they may not realise that they too are members of a ROSCA.

Such groups are found in most regions of the world (Fong and Perrett, 1991, pp. 27-28), and the wide variety of names by which they are known gives some idea of how widespread they are. A small selection of their local names includes: Tontine (Senegal), Susu (Ghana and Trinidad), Gameya (Sudan), Nidhi, Chitty, Kuri, Narukku (India), Palugawan (Philippines), Arisan (Indonesia), Kye (Korea), pia-huey (Thailand), partner (Jamaica), Kou (Japan), Jula-jula (Sumatra), Mengadelek (South Sulawesi in Indonesia), Tanda (Mexico), Box (Antigua), Panderos or Juntas (Peru), Iqqub (Ethiopia), Sana (Dominican Republic), Kameti (Punjab), Chikola (Giriama in Kenya), Piao Hui (Taiwan), Kalanjian (Tamil Nadu) and Stokvel or Gooi-gooi (South Africa). Another common English name is merry-go-round, which graphically describes both the rotating feature and the happiness of receiving the "pot".

The phenomenon appears to be almost universal. In the northern areas of

Pakistan, where the monetary economy has only penetrated since the construction of the Karakoram Highway, and where women are generally not involved in exchanges outside their own households, only one traditional wheat bank was identified in a recent study (Harper A, 1995, pp. 42-43). There is, however, a long tradition of collective agricultural work, and a successful programme of On-Lending Group linkage, with men's and with women's groups, has been built on this foundation.

One reason for the predominance of women in ROSCAs may be their lack of access to more formal systems of financial intermediation. Other marginalised groups, such as immigrant Somalis and Punjabis in London, South Asians in Oxford, Koreans in Los Angeles and displaced Turks in Cyprus, have developed successful ROSCAs as part of their strategy for survival in an alien community (Ardener and Burman, 1995). In South Africa also (Cashbank, 1993), almost everyone is said to be a member of at least one group. ROSCAs, however, are by no means confined to the disadvantaged. Eighty per cent of adults in Taiwan were said to participate in one form or another of ROSCA (Ardener and Burman, 1995, p.2), and 'kitty clubs' are a very common form of social and economic activity among upper middle class women, everywhere.

Opinions differ as to the likely future of ROSCAs. Geertz (1962, p.260) saw them as a temporary phenomenon, being part of the transformation from a particularist to a universalist state of social relations, and he predicted that they would disappear as their functions were taken over by formal financial institutions. This does not seem to have happened, either because his perception was wrong or because the banks have not evolved as they perhaps could and should have done.

As Ardener states (Ardener and Burman, 1995, pp. 2-4), ROSCAs are everywhere, and 'have spread or burgeoned more vigorously than ever". In Cameroon, as in many other countries, informal financial systems which are based on ROSCAs have grown as the formal financial institutions have failed to provide the service people need, and are now themselves evolving into new formal institutions. Rutherford (Rutherford and Arora, 1997, p.9), who has studied financial intermediation in Bangladesh over a long period, states that he found no ROSCAs in Dhaka in 1984, but by 1996 they had almost universal membership.

In Ghana, and elsewhere in West Africa, the promotion of groups, and the collection and management of their funds, has become a business in its own right. In spite of the recent history of high inflation, people are willing to allow a 'Susu collector' to take their daily or weekly savings, and then to receive back the accumulated sum at the end of the year or other pre-arranged period, with no interest added and even with some deduction for the service.

The people who use the same collector may also form a group for social or other purposes, while in other cases they may not even know each other; the relationship of trust is purely between each member and the collector. There are almost 800 registered collectors in the national association, many of whom organise several susu groups, and there are said to be at least the same number of unregistered collectors.

These groups and their susu collectors, however, are beginning to be used by at least one formal financial institution as a channel for savings mobilisation and lending. Citi Savings and Loans Company has recently started what are called Mmoa Bosea, or 'Help Loans' in Accra. These are essentially bridging loans which enable savers to borrow on the security of their future savings. This means that they can access money when they need it and not just at the end of the period agreed with the susu collector. The collector earns a margin on the loans, and is also able to improve his service by offering loans as well as savings facilities, and the loans are guaranteed by the savings of the other members.

These susu groups have between 50 and 300 members, and they also differ from our On-Lending Groups in that they are promoted by the collector rather than by the members themselves; they demonstrate that many types of informal financial intermediary can be used by formal financial institutions to improve their own business and to reach customers who have previously had no access to institutional finance.

Sethi (in Ardener and Burman, 1995, pp. 165-166) quotes a study from as long ago as 1930 which identified 10289 registered ROSCAs in India, of which 4159 were in five districts of Madras Presidency alone. The increasing outreach of financial institutions had a negative effect on their growth, but this was more than offset by women's need for financial services. The numbers of ROSCAs in Kerala and Tamil Nadu doubled annually for some years, and the movement spread from the South of India to the North in the 1950s. Our own study reflects this important difference between the North and the South of India, in that 15 of the 38 Groups which were studied in the South had in some way evolved from ROSCAs, while only two out of 20 in the State of Orissa and none from Uttar Pradesh (U.P.) were found to have originated in this way.

By 1989, however, 35% of a sample of 27 women in the Punjab were found to be members, while Mayoux and Anand (in Ardener and Burman, 1995, p. 176) state that in India ROSCAs are "embedded in village life". Similarly, a 1994 report on women's access to credit in India (SPARC 1995) found "huge numbers of Self-Help Groups in rural and urban India ...unable to tap into the network of funding agencies..." and "often not supported by NGOs...".

This last quotation leads to the issue of the differences between ROSCAs and On-Lending Groups. The members of a ROSCA have to make regular contributions to the common fund, which are either savings or repayments depending on whether the member has an earlier or later turn for the 'pot', and they have to trust at least one of their fellows to organise the meetings and to handle the money or whatever else is collected, even if the whole transaction takes place at one time and there is no need for anyone to retain money that is not hers. They also have to decide on a system for allocating and recording turns, and to agree on simple rules to deal with absence, sickness and so on. Most importantly, they have to remain loyal to the group at least until the end of a complete cycle, even though it is in each member's personal interest to leave as soon as she has had her turn.

An On-Lending Group or micro-bank requires more than this, even if it is not going to borrow outside money. If a group is to accumulate a fund, either for lending to its members or as part-security for a loan, this usually means that no member will be able to enjoy the pot for several meetings, which clearly puts a greater strain on loyalty than when there are payouts at every meeting. On-Lending Groups must also be able to manage a loan portfolio. This is unlikely to be made up of equal loans, on identical terms, to each member, since the essence of intermediation is to balance different requirements. Finally, if a group wishes to lend more money than its members' savings and any accumulated surplus allows, and borrows from a bank or other outside agency, it must also be able to manage the creditor relationship effectively.

A ROSCA can also be completely successful and satisfy all its members even if it survives for only one full cycle. In South Africa, for instance, most of the local stokvels are said (Cashbank, 1993) to be for short-term purposes, such as accumulating funds for Christmas. A genuine micro-bank, on the other hand, can only stop operations when all its loans have been recovered and all its members' deposits or other borrowings fully repaid. This winding up process is difficult. The need for permanence or at least several years' life is perhaps the most fundamental difference between ROSCAs and On-Lending Groups.

These additional requirements clearly demand a great deal more from a group than a simple merry-go-round. The basic goals of the members, the acceptance of regular contributions and loyalty to the group are, however, fundamental features which are probably more important than the additional management and record-keeping skills required for a micro-bank. Worldwide experience, which is supported by the findings of our study, shows that people who have been members of such groups, or come from communities where they are familiar, are well able to take on the additional tasks in spite of obstacles such as illiteracy and inexperience. The poor, it appears, are not only bankable but are able themselves to be bankers.

Pre-existing groups in Kenya

A key feature of local development strategy in Kenya has always been its focus on the local population and its potential. The emphasis is on mobilising and improving local experience and local knowledge, entrepreneurship, and human capital. These should enable communities to harness local resources more efficiently and overcome location, structural or physical disadvantages. Furthermore, in such a strategy, government and other private efforts can be made more effective and relevant to local needs (Alila, 1988).

It can therefore be argued that a crucial requirement in local level development would be the evolution of strong local level organisations. They would act as catalysts for local development initiatives. Development at the local community level requires the presence of strong local institutions. These groups can be used as disseminators of new ideas and innovations, as providers of critical information, and most importantly, playing the role of intermediaries between the people and the government and other development agencies. Community groups have therefore always been encouraged and recognised in Kenya as important instruments in the development process.

It is difficult to estimate the total number of groups in the country, since many are not registered, and some of those which are registered are dormant. In March 1997, the four District Social Development Officers who were visited in the course of this study gave the following as the number of On-Lending Groups in their areas.

In this study, youth groups and women groups are all categorised as On-Lending Groups because the principles on which they were established are not very different from those of the On-Lending Groups. Table 4 confirms the view that there are large numbers of On-Lending Groups in Kenya. The above statistics give an average of almost 2,700 groups per district. If this figure is extrapolated to the whole country, Kenya has 113,400 On-Lending Groups (2,700 On-Lending Groups multiplied by 42 districts). This approximation of the total number of groups in Kenya is not inconsistent with the official 1996 total figure of 63,600 for women's groups obtained from the Women's Bureau of the Ministry of Culture and Social Services.

Table 4: Number of Groups in Four Districts of Kenya

District	No. of groups	Women groups	Youth groups	Total
Meru	2812	1025	-	3837
Nyandarua	2000	1500	250	3750
Kirinyaga	1500	712	-	2212
TransNzoia	70	600	312	982
Total	6382	3837	562	10781

Kenya's population in 1997 was projected to be 29 million, of which the population over 15 years of age was 16 million. The On-Lending Groups which were the subject of this study had an average membership of 20. If every group has 20 members, the total estimated On-Lending Group membership in Kenya is 2,268,000, which is almost 15% of Kenya's adults. This clearly demonstrates the wide coverage of these groups in Kenya.

All the sixteen Kenyan groups which are covered in this study are financially linked with K-Rep, which was not a bank at the time of the field work but was expected shortly to receive a banking licence. None of the groups, however, was actually promoted by K-Rep or any other outside agency, since K-Rep does not perform this function. The majority were formed by small groups of businesswomen, or men, to start merry-go-rounds in order to provide additional capital. Some two or three had moved away from larger groups, and three were started in order to access finance from K-Rep or other agencies.

Pre-existing groups in India

The concept of group activity is traditional in rural India. Historically, there have been groups and groups in the villages, functioning around a particular activity for the common good of their members. In South India, a typical function of such groups was the maintenance of an irrigation tank which served a number of farmers. However, in the post-independence period these informal institutions had gradually disappeared and the village population had started depending more and more on Government intervention to solve their problems.

There are also a large number of affinity groups of people who are engaged in a common economic activity. Some of the On-Lending Groups covered in this study were previously affinity groups, such as cobblers, silk reelers and so on, who had tried to achieve an economy of scale in the procurement of raw material and marketing of their finished products by joining together as a group.

Besides the above groups in which the members come together either for management needs or for common activities and enterprise, there are also large numbers of social, religious and cultural groups which centre around certain religious faiths and social ceremonies and rituals. A few of the On-Lending or Self-Help Groups covered in this study traced their origins to *bhajan mandals* (prayer committees), *mahila sanghas* (women clubs), *yuvak sanghas* (youth clubs) or village *mandals* (village committees). Such groups are generally quite large, and include members who have diverse socioeconomic backgrounds.

Although the members of such groups contribute in cash and kind, their efforts are mostly directed towards a specific purpose, such as going on a pilgrimage, staging a drama, the construction of a temple or management of common resources. Such groups are more common in Karnataka and Maharashtra, as compared to Uttar Pradesh or Orissa. It is significant to note that out of 38 groups studied in Karnataka and Maharashtra, 15 included members who were functioning previously as a group, of which nine were prayer committees. These groups were social or religious groups, which had a limited focus and different and non-financial objectives. Membership had not involved any of the financial discipline which is so important for an On-Lending Group.

There are village committees in almost every village in Orissa, which plan for the welfare of the village. The community usually owns a community hall called "Kothaghara" where the village deity is worshipped; it also performs the functions of a social centre. After harvest, each family contributes a part of their harvest for a common fund, and non-farming families contribute cash. The fund is normally used for religious purposes. If anything remains unspent, it may be used for constructing a school, for renovating a pond, or for other common village welfare activities. Communities also collect other funds, of grain or money, to meet emergencies such as drought or floods. The grain which is stocked in these "golas" can be used by those in need and then has to be returned with some additional quantity of grain; this could be considered the interest.

Except in tribal or lower caste villages, these committees are headed by the members of the upper castes, but they do concern themselves with the welfare of almost all the families in the community. Although they keep reserves of grains or cash to meet emergencies and to cover the cost of religious functions, membership of these Kothagharas does not involve the discipline of regular saving. Furthermore, the lower caste people are not usually required to contribute. These groups are usually large, and they have specific objectives; it might be possible for some such groups to evolve into On-Lending Groups, but they would probably have to split into several smaller sub-groups and this in itself would reduce their cohesion.

In addition to the Kothagara committees, the young people in many villages form youth clubs or "Jubak Sanghas". Many of them are officially registered, and they work on village development tasks such as pond cleaning, forest protection or repairing roads. Some of these groups may have the potential to evolve into On-Lending Groups, although there is no evidence that any have done that so far. One very unusual case is the Janhitaila Sanchaya Samiti, which was started by the village people without any intervention from a bank or an NGO. Janhitaila is a small and rather isolated village in Dhenkenal District of Orissa, quite a poor area, with about seventy households. The community started their seed bank in 1957, and it since that time they have accumulated Rs. 300,000, or over eight thousand dollars. They charge 25% interest on the money they lend; they thus expect every year to accumulate a further Rs 75,000; their fund grows quite rapidly in this way, and they see no need to borrow from formal financial institutions. Many individual villagers, however, have borrowed from Government subsidised schemes such as the Integrated Rural Development Programme. Loan recoveries on such programmes are normally very poor, but there has not been a single case of default in Janhitaila. This is unique in the State, and it shows that community savings and credit activity can not only be successful in its own right, but can be a basis for a strong individual credit culture. It is, however, a very rare example, and such traditional savings groups can usually only be found in remote areas where the pace of socioeconomic development has been very slow.

In the Indian rural scenario, particularly in South India, chit funds, or ROSCAs are ubiquitous. Each member of these groups is required to contribute a fixed monthly amount on a notified date, and the total amount is auctioned among the members at the regular meeting. Whoever bids the highest interest is awarded the chit, and the interest is deducted before the chit amount is given out. The bidder has to repay the principal amount in specified monthly instalments in addition to continuing his monthly contributions. The cycle continues as long as the group wishes.

The number of members depends on the amount which is decided to be pooled and the amount which each member is capable of contributing, and such groups are generally quite large. Economic homogeneity is maintained, since the monthly contributions range from a few rupees to as much as one thousand rupees, or about thirty dollars. The rural bank managers and NGO staff who were interviewed in this study said that as members of these chit funds were already in the habit of saving and inter-loaning, it was comparatively easy to convert them into On-Lending Groups. Although chit fund groups lack the discipline of meetings and the interaction and participation which are so typical of On-Lending Groups, the group members were able to adopt these practices quite easily, so long as the Group members who came from the chit fund group were homogeneous.

There appeared to be no chit funds in any of the villages covered in this study in Uttar Pradesh or Orissa, nor was there any other pre-existing group activity for savings and credit. Chit funds, which are so common in South Indian villages, were conspicuous by their absence. However, chit funds do exist in the urban and semi-urban areas of U.P., and On-Lending Groups can be evolved from such pre-existing groups.

Professional Assistance for Development Action (PRADAN) has promoted the development of several hundred On-Lending Groups around Madurai in southern Tamil Nadu. Most of their members have previously been members of chit funds, which are very common in the area. These groups themselves are not a suitable basis for On-Lending Groups, because they are too large and too impermanent, but the regular savings habit which they have acquired as members of the chits is an excellent background for On-Lending Group membership. PRADAN has found, however, that the pre-existing groups who came together to avoid exploitation when selling their labour can become effective On-Lending Groups much more quickly than groups which have been formed 'from scratch', even when their members have been members of chit fund groups.

Pre-existing Groups—Friends Club

Thirty small-scale vendors and shopkeepers in Narauna, a small town near Aligarh in India, formed a chit fund to help them meet their short-term credit needs. They called it Friends Club. It ran successfully for eighteen months, but it then split into two smaller groups because of some internal disagreements.

Some of the members of one of these groups used to visit the Narauna branch of the Aligarh Rural Bank because they had savings accounts there. The branch manager heard about their chit fund, and persuaded them to convert themselves into a proper self-help or on-lending group, with well-defined rules and bye-laws. He explained the advantages of such a group over their previous loosely constituted chit fund, such as democratic management, more reliable records and the availability of credit from the bank to supplement their own savings.

The members agreed, and their group soon qualified for a loan from the bank. Some members have had problems in repaying their loans to the group, but the group itself has repaid all its instalments to the bank on time.

Conclusion

It would appear, therefore, that group activity of some sort is almost universal, particularly (but not only) among women in poorer communities, and that this necessarily involves a degree of loyalty, discipline and deferred gratification. ROSCAs, merry-go-rounds or chit funds are also common in many areas. These inculcate a regular saving habit, and they introduce members to the concept of financial intermediation, where some people's need to borrow is reconciled with others' ability to save.

On-Lending Groups are not ready and waiting for bank finance in every rural village or urban slum, but many people, and perhaps most women, in poor communities probably have some relevant personal experience of group activity, and in some areas very large numbers have also been involved in informal financial intermediation. This is surely fertile ground for the development of On-Lending Groups as retail marketing links for banks.

2.2. Are Poor People Members of On-Lending Groups ?

Can microfinance eliminate poverty? The aim is to show that poor people can be good bank customers, as savers and borrowers, and that banks can reach them profitably through On-Lending Groups. A banker's job is to make his bank survive and grow, and poverty alleviation is not strictly his business. Nevertheless, it is necessary to know whether very poor people can or do actually benefit from the services of On-Lending Groups. It is obviously a good thing if they do, but one should not exaggerate the impact of this or any other form of microfinance. It is also important not to distort something that is effective in one situation in the effort to apply it to another.

There is of course endless debate as to who the poor are (Bank Poor, 1996, p.9), and unqualified phrases such as "the poorest of the poor" do little to help. In this context, an attempt has been made to find out whether the poorest people in the communities are included in the On-Lending Groups whenever they do operate, and, if so, whether they actually benefit.

One detailed study on this issue was undertaken in northern Pakistan, focusing on the On-Lending Group promoted by the Aga Khan Rural Support Programme (AKRSP). It was found (Harper A, 1995, pp. 85-86) that although AKRSP had insisted that membership of the men's and women's "Village Organisations" should be open to all, the poorest members of the villages were generally excluded. Groups in the smaller villages tended to be more inclusive, and in Gahkuch, a fairly large community, the poorest people were not represented at all in the village organisation (ibid., p.71).

The Village Bank methodology is similar in some respects to On-Lending Groups, except that it demands less of the members, and they are expected to leave after three years, when they reach the maximum loan ceiling of $300 (Holt, 1994, p.157). This might therefore be expected to reach poor people more effectively, but it is said (ibid., p.175) to serve the poor but not the poorest, since the functioning of banks would not be viable if their members were only the poorest people. The less poor are not unnaturally reluctant to include those who are poorer than themselves and therefore seem less likely to be good members.

The Grameen Bank Bangladesh type of group, which facilitates and guarantees for a bank but is not a bank itself, might also be expected to include more of the poorest people than On-Lending Groups, or the ROSCAs from which many of them originate, since the latter demand more of their members and are usually formed by their members rather than by an outside agency with a social agenda. The Grameen Bank, however, and the Bangladesh Rural Advancement Committee (BRAC), are said to be moving away from the 'core poor' (Hulme and Mosley, 1996, p.118) as economic realities overcome the initial purposes of the founders. The poorest people are not only excluded by the better-off, who are reluctant to guarantee their loans, but are also self-excluded (ibid., p.130), since poorer people recognise that they will not be able to cope with the requirements of membership. There does appear to be a rather general problem, if it is a problem, of "client drift" (Harper and Finnegan, 1998, p.65) or "leakage to the non-poor" (Bank Poor, 1996, p.3).

As groups and their members succeed, it is inevitable that some will progress faster than others, and, that the gap between the less poor and the poorest members will increase. One result of this may be that the richer members will 'graduate' to become individual bank customers, and the loan ceilings imposed by the Village Bank programme and other agencies are designed to facilitate this process. Alternatively, if a reasonable number are more successful, the less successful may become marginalised and leave. One group of women brewers in Kiambu in Kenya, for instance, did well and eventually went into the property business. The poorer members however, could not cope with the responsibilities of this development and they left (Geertz, 1962, p.58).

The evidence as to the participation of the poorest people in the type of On-Lending Groups is similar. It certainly does not appear that ROSCAs, or On-Lending Groups, are any more exclusive than other types of groups. A group of practitioners with experience from several Asian countries agreed (Foundation for Development Cooperation, 1992, p.24) that the "vast majority of the target group...(were)... quite genuinely very poor", although they did admit that there was some difficulty in reaching the poorer people because On-Lending Groups were associated with credit unions which themselves were perceived as middle class institutions.

In India, the programme to promote bank linkages with groups in rural areas has been more successful in the richer southern states (NABARD, 1995, p.49), although faster growth was expected in the poorer parts of the country. This may, however, have been related to the long standing tradition of chit funds in the south, rather than to poverty levels as such. Even in the 'heartland' of chit funds, however, the very poorest people seem also to have been excluded. The PRADAN programme of group development in southern Tamil Nadu works in very poor communities, with the landless and low caste people, but even there, the very poorest are generally not members. The PRADAN staff believe that if they were to try to insist that the groups did include the poorest people, the groups would lack the homogeneity that is essential for their success. In urban areas also, On-Lending Group promoters in a British DFID assisted programme have so far generally failed to include the very poor, in spite of attempts to do so (Rutherford and Arora, 1997, pp. 29-30).

Many of the new grassroots microfinance intermediaries which are on-lending bulk funds from SIDBI or from other Indian or international sources also admit that the poorest people are not members of their groups. The slightly better-off members of communities usually resist their inclusion, and the institutions themselves also find it difficult because they want their Groups to maintain regular and high rate of savings, and above all, achieve good recoveries.

It may be worse for the poorest people if they are members, but are not able to take advantage of their membership. In the village of Portu, in northern Pakistan, for instance, the poorest people were members of the village organisations but did not come to the meetings because they could not afford the regular savings contributions (Harper A, 1995, p.61). The proportion of members who had ever taken loans in the AKRSP groups ranged from 25% to 93% (ibid., p.92), but since in these groups the size of loan an individual may take depends on the amount of her saving, the richer members can take bigger loans. Many of these loans were used for farms and other enterprises which generated some employment, usually for the poorer people, so they could enjoy some indirect benefit. Those who do not borrow also benefited from the interest paid by those who did, but this is a relatively small amount.

The AKRSP system also allows people to borrow more than the amount permitted by the level of their savings, if they can persuade other members to pledge their "unused" savings as additional security (ibid., p 102). In general, the poorer members are unable to do this, because of doubts about their repayment capacity. This means that even if the richer people do not have higher than average savings, because they choose to save only the minimum amount, they can still borrow more than the poor.

On-Lending Group membership in Kenya

In the absence of reliable income data or other indicators, the economic status of the members of the groups which were studied in Kenya is examined by reference to the membership qualifications, and their level of education. The types of businesses in which members are engaged also gives some indication of their economic status, since certain activities are unlikely to be undertaken by very poor people.

Every On-Lending Group has certain regulations regarding its membership, which are designed to ensure that every member is seriously committed to the group's activities. The requirements for membership change from time to time in order to exclude people who are not genuinely committed to the progress of the group. At first sight, the membership rules may seem too strict, but experience has shown that this is necessary for the groups' success.

It was reported in the focus group discussions, that the founder members of the groups had established certain criteria which had to be fulfilled before anyone joined the group. Each group had its own set of membership rules, but they were basically very similar. In summary, they all stated that every applicant:

- must be from the locality
- must pay a registration fee (which varies from Kshs. 100 to 1,000, or about US$2 to US$20)
- should be in a known business within the locality
- must be known to other members
- must show a willingness to participate in all the group activities
- must be able to attend all the meetings without fail
- must have a pleasant personality
- should be willing to save with the group
- must be able to contribute the equivalent of what the old members have as savings
- must be dedicated to the group and actively involved in all its activities

- (A requirement of some of the groups) should not to be employed

A small number of the groups also demanded that their members:
- must be women
- must not be in another group
- must not be servicing a loan elsewhere

(Note: here and hereafter, Kenya shillings are converted to US$ at approximately Ksh.55 = $1).

The composition of the groups varies, because they were formed for different reasons, but some of the above requirements show very clearly what kind of membership is required. If all the members have to be in business, they are definitely not the poorest of the poor, since the poorest people in Kenya do not own their own businesses, however small. The membership of the On-Lending Groups that access credit from micro-finance institutions in Kenya is best summed up by the CARE manager who said that the groups they deal with "are those composed of the poorest of the economically active who are in business." All the representatives of microfinance institutions who were interviewed agreed that the members' capital investments were small, but that most of them were above the poverty line.

The groups were generally not socioeconomically homogeneous. When asked whether members came from the same or different social backgrounds, over 80% of the respondents said that group members came from different backgrounds, and 72% also said that some group members are more wealthy than others. This finding is consistent with the general observation that most Kenyan organisations have members from diverse social and economic backgrounds, unless they are clubs for the elite.

According to the 1992 welfare monitoring and evaluation survey, 30% of Kenya's households are headed by women, and 53% of female-headed households in Kenya are poor. This study found that only 15% of the On-Lending Group members were heads of households. The fact that one of the poorest categories of Kenyan households is under-represented in the groups confirms that the members generally are not very poor.

No groups required any particular level of education as a condition of membership.

On-Lending (Self-Help) Group Membership in India

In the stratified society of rural India, people who belong to different castes live in clusters. Generally, the upper caste people live in the centre of the village and along the main thoroughfares, while the lower caste people, who are generally landless, live on the periphery of the village. As one goes around an Indian village, it is very easy to identify the localities where the poor live. In the course of this study people who live in these poor localities were asked if they were members of On-Lending Groups. The results showed that the visibly poorest were generally not members, and in some villages they were not even aware of the efforts that were made by NGOs or banks to form groups in their village.

The group members who were interviewed in the study were asked if they were the poorest people in the village and whether in their opinion there were others who were poorer than them. Invariably the answer was that there were people who were poorer than them. On further enquiry, the respondents said that the poorest people were diffident about joining a self-help group because they were not comfortable with the rigid discipline that was required, nor were they confident that they would be able to save regularly.

Most of the NGO representatives who were interviewed also agreed that the very poorest people were generally left out when groups were being formed. The representative of GMVM in Maharashtra said that their initial efforts to form groups were aimed at all the villagers but the groups which emerged were naturally made up of the people who came forward, and almost invariably, the poorest people were diffident and unwilling. The MYRADA representative admitted that the present groups did not include the poor, but it was felt that as poorer people saw the successful groups of the comparatively better-off, they would come forward to form groups in the near future. The NGOs which are themselves lending to On-Lending Groups also find that the better-off members tend to monopolise the majority of the benefits of membership.

For the purposes of this study landless people were classified as the poorest. Farmers with up to 1 acre of land are classified as poor; and more than 1 acre are classified as better-off . The proportions of each of the above three categories in these groups in Karnataka, Maharashtra, Orissa and Uttar Pradesh were as shown in Table 5. The groups which were promoted by banks are distinguished from those which were promoted by NGOs.

Table 5: Economic Status of Indian On-Lending Group Members

State	No. of groups studied	Total no. of members	Proportion of different categories (%) (Number and %)		
			Poorest	Poor	Better-off
Karnataka NGO	12	248	90 (36%)	46 (19%)	112 (45%)
Bank	13	222	29 (13%)	78 (35%)	115 (52%)
Maharashtra NGO	13	216	82 (38%)	24 (11%)	110 (51%)
Bank	-	-	-	-	-
Uttar Pradesh NGO	6	97	30 (31%)	49 (50%)	18 (19%)
Bank	8	113	20 (18%)	50 (44%)	43 (38%)
Orissa (All Groups)	19	356	56 (16%)	136 (38%)	164 (46%)

These figures are of course not directly comparable with the Indian national figures for the proportion of people below the poverty line, and the definition of poverty is itself a matter of disagreement. Recent changes in the official definition have in fact increased the numbers of "the poor" from around 25% of the population to about 40%. Regardless of precise definitions, however, it does appear that the Indian groups do have a larger proportion of poor members than the Kenyan groups.

Although the groups in Kenya are clients of an NGO, K-Rep, they are in general self-promoted. The comparison between the two countries, as well as the separate data for NGOs and for bank-promoted groups in India, confirms that NGOs, with their intense community contact and a strong social agenda can partly overcome the natural tendency for the poorest people within a community to be excluded both by others and by themselves.

It appears nevertheless, that the poorest people are excluded from microfinance groups, although this exclusion is no more pronounced in On-Lending Groups than any other groups. Various strategies have been proposed to overcome this problem. Some propose that the poorer people need more training in order to give them the confidence and skills to join others who are slightly better-off (Narender, 1996, p.1), while it has also been suggested (Harper A, 1995, p.10) that there may be a need for exclusive groups for the poor in communities where they have been excluded.

On-Lending Groups and the Poor — The Ekta Mahila Mandal
The so-called tribals in India are among the most disadvantaged people anywhere. An NGO organised a group of 50 tribal women in the remote forest area above Chilka Lake in Orissa; the group later split into three sub-groups, on the basis of the small hamlets where they lived.

One of these groups has 21 members. Every household in the hamlet is represented by one woman, and all are equally poor. None of them are literate, and the only criteria are that members should be from the hamlet, and either married or widowed.

The group started by saving five rupees each per week, but they later agreed to reduce this to two rupees, or about six US cents, because of the continuous drought and their general level of poverty. After they had saved Rs. 3300, or about US$ 100, the group received a one-year loan for the same amount from the Puri Rural Bank in Banapur, some 40 kms from their hamlet. Ten of the members took loans; they used the money for small-scale farming in the forest clearings or to finance the collection and sale of "minor forest produce" such as leaves, berries and kindling wood.

The group repaid its loan promptly, and was ready to negotiate a second loan. The members say that they had all been able to reduce their dependence on local moneylenders, and they had also increased their incomes.

Note: Here and elsewhere, Indian Rupees are converted to US$ at the rate of Rs.35=$1.00.

Alternatively, however, it may be that the relative marginalisation which prevents the very poorest in a given community of the poor from being members of groups is part of their poverty, and that there is therefore a need for special programmes for the "core poor" (Hulme and Mosley, 1996, p.113). The "general refrain" of microfinance has been its focus on the so-called poorest of poor, but some agencies, such as the Youth Charitable Organisation (YCO) in Andhra Pradesh in India, have concluded that they are not able to save, and that a quite different grant-based programme may be more suitable for them instead (NABARD, 1995, p.17).

One experienced micro-banker in South Africa (Cashbank, 1993) has commented that when the poorest people are members of groups, they are unable to repay their loans; their inclusion, rather than their exclusion, is the problem. This rather radical view may be a valuable corrective to those who believe that micro-credit can alleviate poverty.

2.3. Must On-Leading Groups have Some Literate Members?

On-Lending Groups are customer-owned micro-banks, which are particularly valuable for disadvantaged women. It seems inconceivable that such a group can operate unless someone can maintain basic records of savings and loans, and explain them clearly and honestly to the membership. Less than half of the adult population of the 48 countries which are classified under the "low human development" category, and which include India and Kenya, can read or write; the female literacy rate in these countries is less than two-thirds of the male rate (UNDP, 1996, table 2, p.139). There seems therefore to be a basic inconsistency between this form of intermediation and the skills of the typical members. Is literacy vital to the success of an NGO, and if it is, how can the problem be overcome?

As already seen, the poorest people, who are presumably those who are least likely to be literate, are not usually members of On-Lending Groups. The problem is nevertheless, a very real one. The shortage of literate women members in the coastal region of Kenya seriously delayed transactions (Bakhoum et al., 1989, p. 61), and in northern Pakistan, where the female literacy rate is under 25% and is one of the lowest in the world, women's groups often find it necessary to appoint a man as their manager (Harper A, 1995, p.86). This is obviously difficult, particularly in a society where any interactions between men and women are subject to so many constraints. The male manager cannot benefit directly from his position, since he is not himself a member. AKRSP, the promoting agency, suggests that managers should be remunerated with a commission of 2% of the portfolio, but the basis of calculation is not clear and the men are in any case reluctant to take the money.

NABARD in India suggested (1995, p.27) that there is a need for an outsider to keep the books if "most of the members are illiterate". In Kalahandi District of Orissa, one of the poorest districts in the whole country, there was apparently only one semi-literate person in an entire tribal community where an NGO was developing On-Lending Groups (Panda and Mishra, 1996). In this situation, it was found necessary for the NGO to keep the records on a semi-permanent basis. It is argued, however, that the groups should use such outsiders only as bookkeepers, and should not allow them also to become managers or secretaries. This can seriously erode the independence of the groups.

There are however some organisations which claim to have overcome the problem. PRADAN offers training in simple bookkeeping for representatives of all new On-Lending Groups. The training is based on the assumption that there will be some illiterates in every group, but it is also assumed that some members will be literate. Their experience has shown that women with no more than three years primary schooling can be trained to keep the records, and to explain them to their fellow-members.

Experience in South Africa suggested that the presence of one or a small number of literates in an otherwise illiterate group could lead to cheating and exploitation (Cashbank, 1993). It was better for the bank to maintain records for the group.

Nine of the 19 groups which were studied in Orissa had no illiterate members at all, and 90 of the total of 356 individual members were illiterate. A number of the groups, including some with literate members, relied on their NGO to maintain their records, and others made use of the services of a literate person from their community, often someone who was still studying.

Literacy is not the same as bookkeeping ability, and there are many very wealthy but totally illiterate people, in both then less-developed and industrialised countries, who are able to maintain control over very large businesses with a minimum of formal skills. An On-Lending group is owned by all its members and not by one individual, and it is therefore important to maintain records, to inform the group as to the state of its affairs and the position of every members' savings and loans. Nevertheless, we should recognise that illiteracy is not as serious a barrier to understanding as literate people may think it is.

The record-keeping system which PRADAN has designed consists only of simple cash book and passbooks for each member, together with a ledger to match the passbooks, and a minute book. All the members have to 'sign' the minutes, in whatever way they can, and they realise that they should not do this until they have fully understood what has been recorded. The Indian Bank branch in Chatrapur, in Orissa, requires the two groups which it has financed, to keep only a savings passbook and a cash book. All the other records are maintained at the bank, and this does not appear to place too great a burden on their staff.

Both the NGO and bank staff who do business with On-Lending Groups stress the importance of records. MYRADA insists that 13 separate books should be maintained, and group members and leaders are trained in bookkeeping soon after the commencement of the group. The manager of the Ittanahalli branch of Canara Bank, Karnataka, who has promoted 22 groups without any NGO involvement, also stressed the importance of proper bookkeeping. He checks the books at every meeting he attends.

The quality of the books of 49 groups which were studied in Maharashtra, Uttar Pradesh and Karnataka were classified as good or poor, using the following three parameters.

(1) Members' satisfaction and confidence in the authenticity of accounts maintained by their group;
(2) The maintenance of at least the most basic books—an attendance register, minutes of the meetings, and savings and loan particulars of individual members; and
(3) Books have to be up-to-date at every meeting.

The results were as shown in Table 6.

Table 6. India—Quality of Groups' Book Maintenance

	Karnataka		Maharashtra	U.P.		
	NGO	Bank		NGO	NGO	Bank
Good	12	11	-	9	5	6
Poor	-	2		1	1	2
Total	12	13		10	6	8
% of good groups	100	85		90	83	75

An attempt was also made to classify the 52 groups into illiterate, functionally literate and literate, as follows:

Illiterate group   -   None of the members have primary education.
Functionally literate group   -   Up to 50% of the members have primary education.
Literate group   -   More than 50% of the members have primary education.

The results of this classification were as given in Table 7.

Table 7. India, Literacy of Groups

State	Total no. of On-Lending Groups studied	Literate groups	Functionally literate group	Illiterate groups	% of illiterate groups
Karnataka	25	2	17	6	24%
Maharashtra	13	-	10	3	23%
U.P.	14	2	10	2	14%
Total	52	4	37	11	21%

All the members of over 20% of the groups were illiterate. Many of these illiterate members had made impressive progress in developing basic numeracy after joining the group, and they had also learnt to sign their names. They took great pride in their ability to do this, and to understand the entries in their passbooks. Within one or two years the attendance registers which used to consist almost entirely of thumb impressions were now completed with neatly inscribed signatures.

The books of the 52 On-Lending Groups which were studied in the three states were maintained by the following people:

Bankers with a banana seller in Orissa, India

On-Lending Group in Bihar, India

Tumaini On-Lending Group in Machakos, Kenya

Members of a Group in Bangladesh

Group leader	35 cases
Another member	2 cases
An outsider	5 cases
NGO worker	10 cases

The Ranabheramma group promoted by MYRADA in Karnataka, which had no literate members, was nevertheless able to function independent of the NGO. The books were kept by the son of one of the members who was a matriculate, and the group paid him Rs. 50 or about US$1.40 per month for this service.

In the functionally literate and literate groups, a total of 53 members had high school education and beyond, and five had college education. Almost invariably these members kept the books of their groups, in addition to being the leaders. There were advantages as well as disadvantages in having one or two educated members. The advantage was that they could be the leaders and keep the books, but this also meant that the other members were dependent on their leader. The members in this situation could not genuinely be considered "empowered".

One of the five groups which employed an outsider to keep its books is only one-year-old, while the other four have been working in this way, quite satisfactorily, for the last three to five years.

There does not appear to be any significant relationships between the quality of the records and the differing literacy levels of the groups, or the people who keep the records.

Table 8 indicates the educational levels of the members in Kenya.

Table 8: Kenya, Members' Literacy Levels by Sex
(The figures in brackets are percentages)

Educational level	Female	Male	Total
None and illiterate	2 (2.7)	1 (1.3)	3 (4.0)
None but can read and write	1 (1.3)	2 (2.7)	3 (4.0)
Lower primary	2 (2.7)	3 (4.0)	5 (6.7)
Upper primary	13 (17.3)	11 (14.7)	24 (32.0)
Lower secondary	7 (9.4)	1 (1.3)	8 (10.7)
Upper secondary	16 (21.3)	12 (16.0)	28 (37.3)
Higher than secondary	1 (1.3)	3 (4.0)	4 (5.3)
Total	42 (56.0)	33 (44.0)	75 (100.0)

Although there is no rule in Kenya which bars the illiterate from group membership, these figures show that very few are actually illiterate. Although the data in the above table are not directly comparable with the national data (Table 9), this does give an approximate indication of the extent to which On-Lending Group members are representative of the whole population. The proportion of group members who have received at least upper primary education, is slightly higher than for the population as a whole, and the educational level of the female members is significantly higher than the national average. This difference may in part be because the national data are for a period of eight years before this study, and during that period primary education has become more available in Kenya, but it supports the conclusion that Kenya's On-Lending Group members are not drawn from the poorest section of the population.

Table 9: Kenya's Population by Sex and Education
(The figures in brackets are percentages)

Level of education	Male	Female	Total
None	1,899,280 (11.3)	2,971,747(17.6)	4,871,027 (28.9)
Primary 1-4	2,238,770 (13.3)	2,074,174 (12.3)	4,312,944 (25.6)
Primary 5-8	2,492,422 (14.7)	2,303,082 (13.6)	4,795,504 (28.3)
Form 1-4	1,227,659 (7.3)	857,088 (5.1)	2,084,747 (12.4)
Form 5 and above	119,842 (0.7)	47,373 (0.3)	167,215 (1.0)
University	58,629 (0.4)	22,939 (0.1)	81,568 (0.5)
Not stated	285,272 (1.7)	265,030 (1.6)	550,302 (3.3)
Total	8,321,874 (49.4)	8,541,433 (50.6)	16,863,307 (100.0)

Source: Central Bureau of Statistics, Kenya Population Census, 1989

In the K-Rep groups, one important reason for the choice of leaders was their literacy. During the focus group discussions, many of the members said that it was essential for the leaders to be able to read and write for them to be able to manage the groups properly. About 60% of the leaders had lower secondary education and above, and only one chairman was completely illiterate; she was, however, supported by an educated secretary. The group secretaries were the best educated; they had all received at least secondary school education, and 16% of them had been educated to the upper secondary level and beyond. The group members felt that this was only right, since they see the secretaries as the custodians of their groups. They keep the records up-to-date, and they are generally perceived as the managers of the groups.

The Problem of Illiteracy—The Ekta Mahila Bachat Samuh

Eleven women in the village of Magdumpur in Unnao District of Uttar Pradesh formed a savings and credit group at the suggestion of the New Public School Samiti, a local NGO whose efforts were supported by the State Land Development Corporation.

None of them is literate, but the daughter of one of the members has been to school and she keeps the books for the group. She reads out what she has written, clearly and loudly so that all the members can hear and understand, and they then put their thumb impressions on the book.

The group's savings amount to about Rs. 3560; they have also accumulated a surplus of Rs. 2800 from the interest they charge on the loans they make, and they have been given a bank overdraft facility of Rs. 10000. They have had no problems with record-keeping.

Conclusion

The problem of illiteracy certainly exists, but it is not insuperable. On-Lending Groups are in themselves a form of adult education, and the simple numeracy skills which are necessary for simple record keeping can be acquired during the period of the group's development. The bookkeeping systems must be as simple as possible, and group promoters should not assume that a group needs the same number and types of books as a full-scale bank does. Illiterate people are often more able to remember facts and figures than those who have come to rely on written records, and there does not seem to be any evidence that the problem of record-keeping has actually stopped On-Lending Groups from succeeding, anywhere.

CHAPTER 3

THE IMPACT OF MEMBERSHIP

3.1. Does Membership Benefit All the Mambers?

There is little doubt that the majority of members of On-Lending Groups benefit from their membership. Studies confirmed that most members' incomes and assets increase, and these quantitative changes are reflected in improved quality of life, increased social confidence, and other manifestations of "empowerment".

Any form of borrowing, or even saving, involves some risk, and poor people are by definition the most vulnerable. Problems such as short-term illness, the death of one animal, or the failure of one crop are relatively minor for better-off people, but such problems can be disastrous for a very poor person. If the loss is compounded with unpaid debt, the situation will be much worse than if the person had not taken a loan at all. We have seen, however, that the poorest people do not usually join On-Lending Groups. Nevertheless, the average member is poor, and it is inevitable that some will fare better than others. The question that must therefore be asked is whether the effect of group membership on some members is to make them worse off than before.

Hulme and Mosley (1996, table 5.1) collected evidence from 11 microfinance programmes which had a similar membership profile to On-Lending Groups, although they were mainly of the Grameen Bank Bangladesh or solidarity group type. They found that the average increases in borrowers' incomes ranged from 1.1% to 44%. Comparative studies of income changes between Grameen Bank members and members of control groups showed that the members were 43% better-off than their neighbours in the same villages, and 28% better-off than similar people in other villages. They also found, however, that the amount of improvement was related to the members' initial incomes; the poorest people benefited either too little, or not at all.

All the members of the AKRSP groups in northern Pakistan (Harper A, 1995) were found to benefit, but the proportionate as well as the absolute improvement to the poorer people's incomes was much lower than for those who were better-off. A study of the impact of On-Lending Group membership in the Philippines covered a sample of 45 members. Thirty eight of them benefited, with income increases from 1% to 100%, but seven suffered decreases, ranging from 8% to 57%. The value of their assets changed similarly.

An impact study of solidarity group lending programmes in Latin America (Otero, 1989, chart 2, p.38) showed that figures of loans disbursed and recovered, even to people in the selected "target", cannot necessarily be equated with increased welfare. It is unreasonable to expect that everyone will benefit equally, or even at all, from group membership, but even lenders who are in the business for profit, and not for development, need to be sure that the costs to the few do not outweigh the benefits to the many.

The study in Orissa found that the poorer members of some groups were unable to maintain the regular savings which were required, or that a few of their families suffered some hardship in order to enable them to save. In some cases the poorer and less active members, who were also illiterate, were quite unaware of the amounts of savings they themselves had accumulated in the group, or of its overall financial position. There was no evidence, however, that their ignorance was being exploited, although this possibility clearly exists.

In a few cases the better-off members of On-Lending Groups were dissatisfied because the group had agreed that all members should have equal loans. The limited savings fund of the group only allowed them to borrow a small amount, and their share was insufficient for the more ambitious projects that they wished to undertake. In contrast, members' savings, and in some cases the funds borrowed from the bank, in the case of six groups, were said to be lying unused in the bank, either because the members had no productive use for more capital, or because they were not aware that the money was available. In the majority of the 20 groups which were studied in Orissa, however, the funds were stated to be fully and equitably utilised.

About one-fifth of the members of the groups in Orissa had not increased their incomes. The others claimed that their incomes had increased by between a third and a half as a result of their membership. They also said that they been able to acquire more household assets, and to improve their food and clothing. They had done this by taking up traditional income-generating activities for which they could previously not afford the necessary capital, by expanding their existing activities, or by paying off expensive loans from moneylenders. A number of groups had also taken up collective activities, such as fish ponds, leasing tamarind trees, paddy processing or growing vegetables.

The social position of the women had also improved; one woman from a group in Pingua that the local bank had promoted, without help from any NGO, said: "Our eyes were closed, now they are open. Now we know our strength."

In Uttar Pradesh, Karnataka and Maharashtra the poorest, those without any of their own land, comprised 29% of the membership. They took 22% of the total value of the loans. This is not entirely equitable, but it is not unreasonable considering their lower absorption capacity; if they had taken larger amounts, they might have been unable to make good use of the finance and would have merely acquired another debt.

The poorer members were asked about the impact of membership on their household assets, and their families' diet and education. The responses are given in Table 10. The poor appear to have enjoyed both tangible and intangible benefits. There was a marked improvement in the value of their movable assets such as dairy animals and of immovable assets, such as minor irrigation works and other forms of land improvement.

More of the sample reported greater improvement in the diet, at 45%, than in assets (32%) or education (16%). This was because they had bought dairy cattle, seeds and fertiliser with the On-Lending Group loans.

These tangible benefits may not be entirely due to the groups, because during the same period household incomes were also increased in other ways such as wages earned by other members of the family and the creation of more jobs in the village as a consequence of land reclamation, and new irrigation.

Intangible benefits are by definition immeasurable, but it was clear that On-Lending Group members' level of confidence, awareness and pride in themselves were substantially increased by virtue of their membership.

Table 10: India: Impact of Group Membership on the Poorest Members

On-lending group promotion (Nos.)	Sample group (poorest members)	Improvement in assets		Improvement in food		Improvement in education	
		Yes	No	Yes	No	Yes	No
NGO (91)	57	14	43	23	34	11	46
Banks (21)	44	18	26	22	22	05	39
Total	101	32	69	45	56	16	85
%		32	68	45	55	16	84

There was also some evidence from Uttar Pradesh in India that group leaders get a disproportionate share of the loans. In Karnataka and Maharashtra there was generally no bias in their favour; the leaders received 15% of the number of loans, and between 8% and 15% of the total amount lent. In U.P., however, the group leaders obtained the major share of the loans (Table 11). This, no doubt, indicates a certain degree of domination by the leaders but they were also usually the better educated and comparatively better-off, so their effective loan absorbing capacity was higher. The poorer members were also sometimes diffident about their repayment capacity and therefore did not apply for loans. They did not wish to risk social ostracism if they were unable to repay.

Table 11. Share of Loans Availed by Group Leaders in U.P., India

Promotion agency	No. of groups studied	Total loans disbursed since the inception of the group (Rs.)	Loans availed by group leaders (Rs.)	Loans availed by poorest members (Rs.)	Loans availed by other members (Rs.)
NGO	6	220372	75398 (34%)	30766 (14%)	114208 (52%)
Bank	8	380645	115475 (30%)	80360 (21%)	184810 (49%)
Total	14	601017	190873 (32%)	111126 (18%)	299018 (50%)

In Kenya the respondents from the microfinance institutions were agreed that the benefits derived by On-Lending Group members do not differ according to their socioeconomic status. The groups generally share whatever resources they have in an equitable way.

In addition to the savings which they made in order to qualify for loans from external agencies such as K-Rep, and their normal loan repayments, all the groups kept up a regular rotating merry-go-round. The Kenya groups were similar in this respect to groups found in other parts of Sub-Saharan Africa. The members of the On-Lending Groups covered in the study were found to be paying monthly contributions ranging from Kshs. 100 to 1,000, or between US $2 and 20. Most groups were paying about Kshs. 200 per month. Although the groups set a minimum amount for the monthly contributions, there was no upper limit and each member could contribute as much as she wished to.

This meant that the On-Lending Groups allowed for the participation of both relatively rich and poorer people. This also allowed groups to be formed in richer as well as poorer areas since the payments were adjusted to whatever people could afford.

The most common way for deciding who is to collect the 'pot' is by drawing lots at the beginning when the group is first formed. That was consistently the method that was used in both the merry-go-round and group-lending activities. New members who join after the start of a group are given turns in the sequence in which they join. These systems are not rigid, however, and the sequence is varied from time to time in accordance with particular members' needs. In a merry-go-round, each member wins on an average about ten times her total contributions. There is, therefore, no element of redistribution, but nor do the better-off members benefit at the expense of those who are poorer. Each benefits according to her ability to save. The routine 'pots', and the K-Rep loans, are distributed without any reference to social, economic or political status.

When the K-Rep funds are distributed, a very clear and transparent method is used to ensure that everybody gets a fair share. Each group elects a loan committee which has to assess each member's business and to determine how much of the loan money each member should get. The only restriction is K-Rep's own rule that the maximum amount for the first loan should be Kshs. 30,000, or about $545, for each member, but members can take as little as Kshs.1,000 if that is what they need.

The above practice is consistent with the policies which have been established (Mutua et al., 1996) for the process by which On-Lending Groups access loans from K-Rep. They stipulate that the group loans committee should visit each applicant to establish what type of business she has and can offer as security to the group for the loan. The committee has to ensure that she genuinely owns the security, and to discuss its appropriateness and acceptability, as well as the family's background, and other issues. The loans committee then makes a written recommendation on each applicant for presentation in the next meeting. The committee is elected by all the members, and this process ensures that it serves all the members fairly.

Over half of the respondents in the study had received at least two loans, and over ninety per cent said that they had benefited from the loans. Three per cent of the members said that they did not benefit from the loans because the first loan was too small, and one member complained that all the profit that she was earning from her business was being used to repay loans owed by defaulters in her group.

The Impact on Members—the Devthala Village group

The Oriental Bank of Commerce set up a project to introduce thrift and credit groups to fourteen disadvantaged villages in the Himalayan mountain area of northern Uttar Pradesh. The project manager chose to work first in Devthala, the poorest of the villages. The people there were very mistrustful of outsiders, because they had often been cheated before, and the manager had first to ingratiate himself with the village priest before they would accept him.

He eventually persuaded five women to start; three of their husbands did their best to prevent the group from starting, and even physically threatened the manager, but he was not discouraged. The bank arranged some training for the members, and they were able to finance new activities such as knitting, ginger farming and pickle making with the loans they received from the group. They started with loans as small as Rs. 75, or about US$2, but within two years they have borrowed up to Rs. 15000, or US$430.

The average incomes of the five women increased by over 40%, and two of the poorest of them, who had previously been forced into prostitution because of their desperate need, had purchased dairy cattle and started some small-scale farming. They now enjoy the respect of their fellow-villagers.

Following the success of this first group, thirteen more groups were started, covering all the 92 families in the village. They have accumulated savings of over US$3000, and have borrowed a total of twelve thousand dollars from the bank. Forty-two further groups have been started in neighbouring villages, and the bank's savings and loan business with On-Lending Groups is growing much faster than the rest of its business in the area.

Conclusions

It is always difficult to find out how the less successful participants in any activity are faring, and most work is focused on the success stories. The evidence suggests, however, that nearly all the members of On-Lending Groups benefit to some extent, although the benefit to the poorer members may be less, and longer-delayed, than to the better-off. It is perhaps inevitable that those who are least in need should be the ones to gain the most, but in India in particular the majority of the members of most groups are very poor, and benefits to any of them represent genuine social progress.

Such inequity as it exists appears to be rather more pronounced in India than in Kenya, perhaps because the members of the Kenya groups are in general rather higher in the socioeconomic scale than those in India. Bankers may be confident, however, that the profitable business that they can generate through On-Lending Groups is not being gained at the expense of social equity.

3.2. What About Those Who Drop Out ?

In examination of the welfare effects of group membership, the issues that have been dealt with are whether the poorest are excluded, and whether all the people who are included actually benefit from their membership. What remains is perhaps the most difficult question, which concerns those who may be the worst sufferers. These are the "drop-outs"; people who for some reason cease to be members. Are there many of them, and what is the impact of their experience?

People who leave a group, whether voluntarily or because they are compelled to, are almost by definition difficult to find. They may have left the area, or they may have sunk below the level of their ex-colleagues' attention, or indeed risen above it. If they have failed, this is also a failure for the group, and for the promotion agency or bank, so they will naturally be reluctant to talk about them. If they can themselves be found, they too may be unhappy to talk about their own failure. Attempts to find out about drop outs from South African programmes have been frustrated because the people concerned tend to leave the urban townships and return to their home villages, where they cannot be traced (Cashbank, 1993).

There is therefore little published material on drop-outs, although awareness of the problem is growing, and as with earlier issues, most of what is available relates to Grameen Bank type groups rather than to On-Lending Groups in our sense.

Hulme and Mosley have uncovered a certain amount of evidence on this topic in their detailed study of eleven microfinance programmes throughout the world (1996, pp. 121-122) . They found, for instance, that in the TRDEP programme in Bangladesh some 20% of members drop out before their third loan, "usually the most vulnerable who drop out as a result of failing to use the loan successfully". The annual drop-out figure for Grameen Bank is apparently about 15%. There have also been isolated cases of members of the Grameen Bank committing suicide, at least partly because of their debt burden, and group members have been known to tear down a defaulter's hut.

The drop-out rate from BRAC was said to be 16% in 1992 and 10% in 1993 (Montgomery, 1995, p.9), and the researcher's "impression" was that most of them drop out because they cannot cope with the strict savings and repayments requirements, and most of them are from among the poorest members. BRAC's strict policy of avoiding consumption loans has also contributed to the drop-out rate.

ASA, is one of the largest but also less well-known microfinance institutions in Bangladesh, and has some 400,000 members, organised on a similar system to the Grameen Bank or BRAC methods. They carried out a study (ASA, 1996, pp. 41-42) into the reasons for drop-outs, and found that the main reason given by members and staff was the institution's strict ceiling on the amount and number of loans which one member could have. Repayment difficulties and dislike of the collective responsibility and discipline required of members of the programme were the second and third most frequently mentioned causes.

These difficulties do seem in part at least to be related to the design of the programme itself, and "top down" programmes of this type, where the members work in groups which come together and operate according to a strict set of rules, are said to encourage an insensitive approach to dealing with late payers. In contrast, the SANASA system in Sri Lanka, which has revived village cooperatives, and where many groups effectively operate as On-Lending Groups, is said to have far more humane and no less financially viable methods of dealing with the problem. The groups design their own repayment schedules, rather than having to adhere to a strict standardised timetable irrespective of their household cash flows.

There are few drop-outs from the groups in northern Pakistan (Harper A, 1995, p.61), but there are isolated cases. In the village of Portu, for instance, one woman who could not repay was expelled from her group after her savings had been seized. This not only deprived her of further access to the financial services of her Village Organisation, but it also meant she could no longer participate in its no-financial activities.

There are some withdrawals from the Village Bank system (Holt, 1994, p.172), but these are said mainly to occur because some members have no need for further loans, and not because of problems with saving or repayment. Some of these voluntary drop-outs return to the groups when they need to borrow again.

The literature of microfinance is replete with heart-warming micro-case studies of success, describing how destitute people have overcome their problems with the help of credit. Given here is information about some cases which tell the other side of the story.

Figures were obtained in Orissa for the change in membership numbers since the formation of the 19 groups which were studied. Four had increased their membership, six had remained the same, and nine had decreased. The total number of members had decreased from 428 to 356, and 115 members had withdrawn, while 43 had joined. Two of the reductions had taken place because the groups, with 50 and 86 members, had proved too big to manage, and they had split into smaller groups. They were in any case far above the maximum number of about 20 which is recommended to banks which take refinance from NABARD for on-lending to groups. The figures are not inconsistent with the average drop-out rate of 10% which other Indian microfinance institutions have experienced in the groups which they have financed (SIDBI, 1997).

The other reasons for withdrawal are :
- some members could not spare enough time for the group meetings
- there were disagreements within the group
- some members died
- some members moved to another village
- some members were not committed to the group and could not or would not maintain regular savings.

Some of these reasons may of course conceal hardship or poverty, but it is significant that late payment was not mentioned as a specific reason for withdrawal by any of the groups. There were problems of arrears in several groups. In one group with 28 members, ten members were in arrears and the secretary had to go round to their houses every month to collect payments because the defaulters were reluctant to attend the meetings.

In another case, four members left because their families did not want them to belong to the group, and a fifth withdrew voluntarily after she had had difficulty in repaying a loan for Rs. 4000. After being under some pressure from the other members she finally repaid the full amount plus interest, but she then decided to withdraw. The rest of the group allowed her, and the other women who had withdrawn, to take all her accumulated savings, and her share of the accumulated profit. Most groups adopted the same practice when people withdrew, but some only repaid savings and did not allow departing members to take their share of the groups' profits.

It proved possible actually to interview 17 people who had dropped out of groups in Orissa. They were asked whether they had joined a new group, and whether their economic status had suffered after leaving. Four people had left to join a new group, and of the remaining thirteen, ten said they were worse off than before.

A detailed study was undertaken in Uttar Pradesh in an attempt to find out when members withdrew from their groups. It was found that the majority of the drop-outs occurred during the early life of the group, and this was generally part of the usual process of "storming" which follows the initial "forming" and precedes "norming" and "performing", in the accepted model of the four stages of the group formation process. These drop-outs took place because of disagreements among the members and some members' unwillingness to accept others as leaders. Family problems such as the need to look after children or old and infirm people at home sometimes prevented members, particularly women, from attending meetings.

Detailed analysis of the membership registers of the On-Lending Groups in Uttar Pradesh showed that most later drop-outs after the first year of a group's life took place due to women members getting married and leaving the villages. Otherwise drop-outs took place in the initial stages of group development, usually during the first year.

The reasons for drop-outs in different stages of the group cycle for the groups in U.P. are given in Table 11.

Table 11: Reasons for Drop Out of Members in U.P., India

Reasons for drop out	Numbers dropped out	
	Formative stage (up to 6 months)	Post-formative stage (above 6 months)
Inability to save and attend meetings	8	-
Residing at a distant place	3	1
Disagreement on rules/bye-laws	1	2
Difference in socioeconomic status	2	-
Migration	-	6
Total	14	9

Drop-outs in Kenya

Over 90% of the Kenyan Group members who were interviewed said that their groups have experienced exits since they were formed, but 80% of the respondents considered the turnover not to be very high. Some groups have not lost any members at all, while others have lost as many as half their members. As Table 12 shows, most groups have kept the drop-outs to less than 20%. Some clients have left the groups voluntarily, but others were expelled, usually as a result of default. The average default rate on first loans was just over 7%, excluding one exceptional case where the default rate was over 80%.

Table 12: Kenya: Analysis of Exits and Defaulter Rates

On-Lending Group	First K-Rep loan	Members at time of first time	Current members	% Drop out	1st loanees	1st defaulters	% of 1st defaulters	2nd loanees	2nd defaulters	% of 2nd defaulters	3rd loanees	3rd defaulters	% of 3rd defaulters
Kaaga	1995	30	19	36.7	19	3	15.7			-	-		
Kerugoya	1994	16	13	18.7	16	1	6.2	13	10	76.9	-		
Kyeni	1996	20	20	0	20	5	25.0	-	-	-	-		
Marigo	1995	21	20	4.7	12	2	16.7	10	0		-		
Mitumba	1995	30	25	16.7	30	1	3.3	25	0		-		
Tumaini	1995	24	15	37.5	24	0	0	12	0		-		
Wihoke	1995	18	18	0	18	15	83.3	-	-		-		
Zaburi	1996	20	19	5.0	19	0	0	19	0	0	-		
Gichira	1993	30	15	50.0	30	0	0	30	3	10.0	-		
Kugiwa	1993	27	21	22.2	27	0	0	27	0	0	21	3	14.2
Muthinga	-	-	19	-	30	4	13.3	23	2	8.7	-	-	-
Mwija	1994	25	5	80.0	25	3	12.0	9	4	44.4	-	-	-
Wanyua	1994	27	27	0	28	0	0	27	0	27	19	3	15.7

From Table 13 a clear trend emerges whereby membership reduces as the groups continue to receive loans from K-Rep. While the group membership averaged nearly 24 at the time they joined the K-Rep programme, it has currently dropped to 18. The number of those taking loans is also steadily decreasing as they move from the first loans onwards. The analysis shows that on an average 23 members took first loans while only about 20 took second loans.

Table 13: Kenya: Average Number of Loanees and Defaulters

Variable	Mean	Minimum	Maximum	Std. deviation
No. of members at intake	23.73	16	30	5.08
No. of current members	18.07	5	27	5.18
No. of 1st loanees	22.92	12	30	5.98
No. of 1st loan defaulters	2.62	0	15	4.09
No. of 2nd loanees	20.56	9	30	7.62
No. of 2nd loan defaulters	2.37	0	10	3.46
No of 3rd loanees	20.00	19	21	1.41
No. of 3rd loan defaulters	3.00	3	3	3.00

The first loan is used as a screening device to identify those who are serious borrowers and those who are not. The group members show their real character during the period of the first loans and this gives the members and K-Rep a practical opportunity to find out which members can be relied on. Membership is therefore quite often reduced after the group finishes with its first loan, because members who are not serious withdraw at that time.

The members who leave the groups voluntarily were said not to be worse off than before. Some have found the group meeting obligation too inconvenient, others are unwilling to co-guarantee their fellow-members' loans while others withdrew because their savings had been used to repay defaulters' obligations.

Although it was not possible to trace people who had left the groups, some information was obtained from the remaining members of the Mwija and the Gichira groups, the two worst groups, as to why the drop-outs had left. A summary of the reasons is given here.

Exits from Mwija On-Lending Group

1. Cecilia Ngure left the group in 1995. The other members rejected her because she used to delay her repayments and rarely attended group meetings. It was reported that she is still in business.
2. Grace Wanjiku left in 1995. She was rejected by the other members because of delays in repayments and non-attendance at meetings.
3. Paul Kamau left in 1995. He defaulted and was unable to repay his loan. He consequently closed down his business.
4. Stella Mwari resigned from the group in 1995. She was unable to attend meetings monthly.
5. Stella Kagweria defaulted in 1995. Her business was doing very poorly and she could not repay her loans.
6. Cecilia Kathure was unable to repay her loan and she closed down her business in 1995.
7. Trisposa Kiunga resigned from the group in 1995 because she was not able to attend the meetings.
8. Harun Mwagaju was unable to repay his loan in 1996. His business was doing very poorly.
9. Samson Kinyua resigned from the group in 1995 citing his inability to meet the group's requirements and conditions.
10. Eunice Kaimuri left in 1995. Immediately she received her loan, she abandoned the group and was never traced.
11. Domiano Mbaabu left in 1995 because his business was doing poorly. He therefore had repayment problems. He consequently abandoned the group and his business closed altogether.
12. Joseph Mwamba defaulted in 1995. He closed down his business because it was doing poorly.
13. Jacob Mukindia resigned in 1995 because he did not have the time to attend the meetings.

14. Daniel Mburugu defaulted in 1995 because his business was doing poorly so he could not repay his loan. He subsequently closed down the business.
15. Rose Kinya left in 1995 because she had difficulties in repaying her loan. She relocated her business and has not been seen since.
16. Esther Mugambi ceased to be a member in 1995 because she never attended the meetings.
17. Joseph G. Japhet lost his membership in 1995 due to his failure to attend meetings.
18. Lydia Mutca also lost his membership in 1995 due to non-attendance
19. Naomi Nyoroka ceased to be a member in 1995 due to non-attendance at meetings.
20. Daniel Muthuri stopped in 1996 due to non-attendance at meetings.
NB. Those who were not attending meetings were asked to leave the group even though their loan repayment were up-to-date. Non-attendance at meetings was viewed as a sign of lack of commitment to the group.

Exits from Gichira On-Lending Group

1.   Kafue wa Waguma left in 1997. He neither saved with the group nor did he pay the group penalties. His business was also doing very poorly.
2.   Nyoroka left in 1997 after she realised that K-Rep was not going to make another loan to the group although she had continued to make savings (the group had not yet finished repaying K-Rep's earlier loan).
3.   Wanjiru Nderitu experienced a low spell in her business in 1997 and she quit the group. She also had difficulties in repaying her loan.
4.   Mwaniki left the group in 1997 due to her inability to comply with the group's rules.
5.   Njaramba left the group in 1997. He was a teacher and had registered his wife with the group to get a loan. He had difficulties in repaying the loan because he had no business. He defaulted and quit the group.
6.   Karini left the group in 1997. His business was doing badly due to the weather and he was therefore unable to repay. He could not even contribute to the group's savings.
7.   Njoki left in 1997. Since the group was not able to borrow from K-Rep due to the problem it had with defaulters, she thought that she was wasting her time with the group. She therefore quit.
8.   Mary left the group voluntarily in 1997. She was comfortable with the income she was getting from her business.
9.   Wanja left the group in 1997 after she realised that K-Rep was not going to give it a loan.
10. Titus passed away in 1995.
11. Irene defaulted in 1995. She has made no effort to repay her loan, and cannot be traced.

12. Mulei left after receiving his second loan. He cannot be traced.

13. Wanduma defaulted in 1996. His savings were not enough to cover his loan balance. He has not yet returned to the group to let them know why he was unable to repay his loan.

14. Mwangi was unable to repay his loan in 1996 and requested that his savings to the group be used to pay off his loan balance.

15. Wamaitha was unable to repay his loan in 1996. Even though his savings were used to offset the loan, he still has an outstanding balance of Kshs. 2000. He closed his business because it was doing very poorly.

16. Paul Ngure quit the group in 1995 voluntarily.

Members who left because of non-attendance at meetings may have failed to turn up because they could not make the repayments, or the expected savings contributions. The brief descriptions given in the boxes suggest however, that defaulters are noted as such. If this is the case, it appears that 19 of those who dropped out of these two groups left because their businesses were doing badly and they could not repay their loans, while 19 left because they felt they were not benefiting from their membership, and did not want to spend time going to meetings.

Some of the groups have faced serious defaulter problems. The Wihoke Ngwihoke group had a default rate of 83.3% on their first loan. Kerugoya Umoja had a default rate of 76.9% and Mwija recorded 44% on their second loans. The trend that seems to emerge is that the default rate goes down as the loan amounts increase. This is to be expected because the first loan serves as a selection mechanism, and those who are less committed to the group fall out at this time. It is also the first experience of loans for most of the group members and they can easily make mistakes in their use of the loans and thus be unable to repay. As they take more loans, their financial management skills improve and they are less likely to default.

On-Lending Groups that are experiencing a high rate of default are on the verge of disintegration, and it is obvious that these groups are performing worse as groups than before they were linked with K-Rep, even though most of the individual members and their businesses may be doing satisfactorily. Wihoke Ngwihoke which is one of the groups with the highest default rate no longer carries out many of the activities it used to do before collaborating with K-Rep. Most of the members have lost their savings because they have been used to repay defaulted loans.

During the focus group discussions, the members said that people who had defaulted and left their groups had ended up much poorer than they were before they joined the credit programme. They explained that most of those who had defaulted had closed their businesses altogether. As one succinctly put it "defaulting is an indication that they are not doing well in their business. That is because if they were doing well, then repayment would not be a problem."

During discussions with the leading microfinance institutions in Kenya, it was apparent that defaulters have always left the programme much worse off than when they joined it. It was clear, however, that the defaulters are those who take loans without proper plans on how to use them. They invest the money in unproductive ventures and thus cannot repay. The group members agreed, and said that those who take loans without proper planning always end up as defaulters.

Drop-Outs; Case 1—Joseph Muna Karuciu

Joseph Karuciu started his greengrocery business in 1993 at Soko Mjinga in Nyeri town. He joined the Amani Group in 1994. The group was started in May 1994 with 53 members, and joined K-Rep in 1994 with 30 active members.

Joseph received his first loan of Kshs. 5,000, or about US$ 90, in November 1994, to be repaid within six months. He profitably invested the whole amount in his business. He successfully finished repaying this loan in May 1995. In July 1995, Karuciu took a second loan of Kshs. 15,000, with which he bought a lorry load of vegetables. When he brought the produce to the market, he found that prices had fallen steeply and he had to sell the vegetables at a loss. He was thus unable to service his loan and the group repaid it for him. But he still repays the group whatever he can.

Joseph says that the first loan really helped him to improve his business and he was able to use part of his profits for his family. When he realised that he was unable to service the second loan, he voluntarily resigned. The group understood his problem and were willing to cover the balance from their savings. Even though he is now only repaying the group quite slowly, he hopes to be able to clear the balance eventually.

He confirmed that his business was not performing as well as it used to before he took the second loan. But he attributed the change to poor business timing. He was of the opinion that with better timing on his part, the business would not have gone down as it has.

Drop-outs, Case 2 — Purity Wairimu Wambui

Purity Wambui sells fruits in Nyeri. She is a member of Mageria On-Lending Group which was started in 1994. She joined the group when it had 30 other members. The group joined K-Rep in 1994.

Purity received her first loan of Kshs. 10,000, or about US$ 180, in 1994. She used the money to buy potatoes which she sold at the market. Her business expanded, and she finished repaying the loan within six months. She took her second loan of Kshs. 25,000 in 1995, and bought 28 bags of potatoes at Kshs. 600 per bag during the rainy season. Unfortunately, when she came to sell them, she found that the market had been closed by the Municipal health department because of its poor sanitary conditions. She was only able to sell two bags at a good price and had to sell off the remaining 26 at a loss. She had spent about Kshs. 20,000 of the loan money, so she started repaying the loan with the balance of Kshs. 5,000. She struggled to repay the loan for 11 months but she still had an outstanding balance of Kshs. 5,000.

Purity willingly resigned from the group in April 1996. She said that her business was doing very badly and she was constantly in arrears with the loan repayments. She still hoped to clear her remaining balance with the group. She admitted that ever since she took the second loan, her economic status had got worse, but she blames the municipal authorities whose decision to close the market coincided with her purchase of a large stock with the loan money.

Conclusions

It is clear that a number of On-Lending Group members drop out of the groups, many of them involuntarily, and that their financial position, and presumably their own and their families' general economic and social condition are then worse than before they joined. The same could of course be said for the clients of any financial institution, and there is no reason to suppose that the overall proportion of failures is any higher than in a typical bank's portfolio of small business customers.

We are dealing, however, with vulnerable people, and although it is unreasonable to expect everyone to benefit, we must ensure that there is nothing particularly damaging in the system of intermediation we are promoting.

The limited evidence from the experience of programmes using Bangladesh Grameen Bank type solidarity groups seemed to suggest that systems with a direct relationship between clients and the lending institution, without the intermediation of a On-Lending Group, may be less sensitive to the problems of potential defaulters. Our own evidence from Kenya and India confirms that there are substantial numbers of drop-outs, but it also shows that their problems arise more from the exigencies of business than from any factor related particularly to their membership of a group. It would be foolish to suggest that any particular retail source of financial services could eliminate or even significantly reduce the ordinary risks of business. On-Lending Groups can, however, enable banks to provide poorer people with access to the same sort of service that others enjoy, with the same risks.

3.3. Does Outside Money 'Spoil' the Groups ?

Although a minority of On-Lending Group members may not benefit as much as the majority, and some may suffer as a result of their membership or of losing it, there is little doubt that the majority of members do benefit from the financial services that they obtain from their group. In Orissa, 80% of the members who were interviewed said that they were earning more than they had before they joined, and most of them had also been able to clear their debts to moneylenders. Within one to two years, they had been able to increase their incomes by 30% to 50%.

Similar results were reported from the other Indian states, and from Kenya, and these figures are typical of findings from elsewhere.

The concern here, however is not the immediate impact on the members of the On-Lending Groups, but the impact on the groups themselves. Bankers and other lenders, like any supplier who distributes his product through independent retail outlets, must ensure that these outlets remain viable and effective. The very attraction of the product to the final consumers may even place intolerable strains on the management or finances of the intermediary. The members and owners of a On-Lending Group are of course also its customers, but it is still important to distinguish between the two entities.

Here again, much of the published evidence relates to solidarity groups rather than On-Lending Groups. One possible problem which can arise from the very success of microfinance is highlighted in "Empowered to default", Yaqub's paper (1995, p.4) on his findings from BRAC in Bangladesh. Some successful women borrowers have apparently become as "empowered" as many richer males have always been, in that they feel secure enough not to repay. If this phenomenon was common in On-Lending Groups, any prudent lender would obviously avoid a form of intermediation which has built into it the seeds of its own destruction.

There would certainly appear to be a possibility that groups will take outside money less seriously than their own members' savings. Successful lending and recovery from their own fund might not be sufficient evidence that they would behave in the same way with funds from another institution. Loans from credit unions, for instance, are "almost entirely financed by member savings, not by external donations or loans" (Magill, 1994, p.147), and it is suggested that this explains their generally successful record.

There is also the issue of management. A group which has successfully managed a merry-go-round, or has lent and recovered funds from its own resources, will not necessarily be able to cope with the more demanding requirements of a larger portfolio, and the task of managing the relationship with a formal institution. In South Africa (Hulme and Mosley, 1996) it was found that some On-Lending Groups could not transfer their undoubted skill at managing small sums to the management of larger loans, with longer repayment terms.

There is some evidence, however, which suggests that genuine intermediaries such as On-Lending Groups may be less likely to be "polluted" by outside money than solidarity groups on the Grameen Bank model, which are also the basis of BRAC's system. The Village Bank model (Holt, 1994, p.171) involves cheap loans or even grants as initial capitalisation. The repayment experience has generally been good, although groups which have been charged low interest rates for their initial capital have tended to perform worse than those which have paid something nearer to commercial rates.

It is very easy for outside observers to confuse intermediating On-Lending Groups with solidarity groups, and this confusion can also affect the behaviour of the groups themselves (Fernandes, 1992, p.63). Banks must avoid weakening group solidarity by implying that their loans are for individual members, even if the amount of the loan is calculated and approved by identifying, appraising and aggregating the requirements of each member. The loan is to the group, not to the individual members, and if they understand this they will be more likely to feel their group responsibility to repay.

The experience of some urban groups in India suggests that the possibility of outside money can also act as a selection device (Rutherford and Arora, 1997, p. 25). Some weaker groups in the cities of Vijayawada and Cochin, which had started on the promise of grants, collapsed when the grants did not materialise as easily as their members had hoped. Other more strongly-based groups persevered when the grants were not forthcoming, and even saved more money themselves than the grant would have provided. They thus became well qualified to take loans on a commercial basis.

Disadvantaged people, for whom any form of institutional finance other than charitable grants was previously inconceivable, may also gain in self-respect if their own group is considered worthy of a loan. A group of leaf-plate makers in Sirpur, in India, increased their rate of savings and the solidarity of their group, after they had taken a loan from Friends of Women's World Banking (Rutherford and Arora, 1997, p.24). PRADAN in southern Tamil Nadu have also observed that the availability of outside money can enhance a group's confidence and self-respect, so long as the terms, the timing and the amount are correctly judged. The NGOs funded by SIDBI have also found that when On-Lending Group members receive money from outside they are forced to take the management of their own and their groups' financial affairs more seriously. This strengthens mature groups, but it may damage groups that lack the necessary management skills, and the capacity to use the money effectively. The timing is critical.

The twenty groups which were studied in Orissa had generally benefited from the loans which they had received, both as groups and as individual members, but there were inevitably some problems which had arisen. The two most common, each of which was mentioned by four groups, were their increased dependence on the NGO which had facilitated their access to the outside finance, and their failure to make use of all the funds they had.

This latter problem seems to have arisen either because of the member's lack of good ideas for investment, or, more often, because the members were not really aware of how much money the group had. In one case the Secretary was using all the money herself, without informing her fellow members, but in the other three cases the problem seemed to be a matter of lack of understanding rather than misinformation.

Members of one other group reduced the amount and regularity of their savings, because they felt that the bank loan meant that it was no longer necessary to accumulate their own funds. There was also one case where a large On-Lending Group had been broken up into two smaller groups because the bank took a legalistic view of the official tax regulations regarding the size of groups, and insisted that they would not entertain loan applications from any group with more than 20 members.

One clear result of the larger sums which were available to On-Lending Groups from bank loans was the shift from consumption loans to loans for productive investments. The distinction is of course not a clear one; money spent on medicine to enable a sick person to return to work, or on food which helps to prevent wage earners from getting sick or gives them energy to work, has as high an economic rate of return as most so-called "productive" investments.

The proportion of loans which were taken for "consumption" by group members in Karnataka, Maharashtra and Uttar Pradesh fell from 80% in the first year of the groups' existence to 44% in the second and later years, and the amount spent on productive investments rose by a far larger proportion. Members presumably made this shift because their improved economic position meant that they were able to satisfy their immediate needs without borrowing, and could "graduate" to larger longer-term investments. This suggests that the overall position of the members, and their On-Lending Group, benefited as a result of their access to additional funds.

The negative impacts in Kenya

The On-Lending Groups which are linked to K-Rep were all set up by their members with little or no intervention or assistance from K-Rep itself, and most of them had been in existence for some time before they had even heard of K-Rep. They therefore usually had to make some rather fundamental changes in their operations in order to reflect K-Rep's focus. If a group was only operating a merry-go-round, and did not save any of its members' contributions, it had quickly to start saving in line with K-Rep's requirements. This has meant that over a period of time, most groups have stopped their other activities and are only engaged in savings towards their next K-Rep loan, and in managing the loans they have already taken. They have generally stopped saving for their own fund, and many groups actually refer to their savings as "K-Rep savings".

A closer look at those that still carry out the group saving activity revealed that it is widely perceived as a cushion against possible defaulters. The same reason has led to the rise of what groups refer to as emergency funds whose actual purpose should have been to help members who had urgent needs for money for purposes such as funerals, weddings, school fees and so on, but which are now being increasingly looked at as a reserve in case any of the members default. Although they have not completely stopped other activities which are geared towards mutual support, these have become peripheral. Indeed, most of the groups which have default problems tend to stop all their other activities and instead to concentrate only on loan repayments until the situation has improved.

This supports the view that the groups are increasingly losing their autonomy as a result of their collaboration with microfinance institutions. CARE Kenya stated that some of the groups have lost their autonomy and only concentrate on their savings and lending, and some of them are even calling themselves "CARE groups". Kenya Women Finance Trust agreed that this was happening to some groups, but only to the weaker ones. Once those groups start losing their autonomy they cease to strive towards sustainability.

The impact of K-Rep's assistance to the On-Lending Groups has also had other adverse effects on them. Most of the groups have lost some of their group savings as a result of member defaults. Once a group's savings have been seized by K-Rep, or have been used by the members to offset an outstanding loan balance, this always sets a bad precedent. As the members of the Kerugoya group said, using savings to pay for defaulters encourages others to stop repaying their loans too. This has led to members being increasingly reluctant to contribute their savings to the groups. The capital base of the groups is thus eroded, which in turn leads to general apathy towards group activities and withdrawal of members.

The Gichira Group in Nyeri had to use about $ 2,000 from their group savings to pay for defaulters, and it almost disintegrated because the members were disillusioned. The 15 members who remain from the original 30 said that had it not been for K-Rep, the membership would still be intact.

The disorganised way which some groups manage their loan repayments has also caused trouble to their members. There is no way in which the members can force their officials to confirm to them whether they have remitted loan repayments to K-Rep's or not. In some groups, the leaders show the bank slips to the members at their meetings to confirm that they have indeed banked the money, but in others the leaders decide not to do this. If the K-Rep Credit Officer does not constantly monitor the group, it can take some time before the members discover that the group's repayments have not been remitted to the bank, and during that time the group can lose thousands of shillings.

The Wihoke Ngwihoke Group in Nyandarua is a good example of how the loan repayment procedures can be manipulated so that the funds are misappropriated. For over five months, the members gave their loan instalments to the group's leader, but she never forwarded the money to K-Rep. Eventually, she disappeared. The members felt that they had lost their money through no fault of their own, and they blamed K-Rep for their loss. The Thika Gwikuria, Gichira, and Kerugoya Umoja On-Lending Groups have also had similar problems; their members now believe that their association with K-Rep has not helped them, but has only led them to make losses.

Some of the group members experienced domestic problems because of the pledges they had made for loan security. They mentioned land title deeds and licenses for electronic equipment such as television sets. The members complained that their spouses were not happy that although they had themselves completely repaid their loans the certificates could not be released because the other members had not cleared their loans. They blamed this on their group's collaboration with K-Rep.

Some of the On-Lending Groups lost members because they could not cope with their loan repayments. As the groups changed from being essentially social organisations and concentrated only on savings and lending, members who were unable to participate in the new activities had to leave. These members were thus deprived of the social security that they had enjoyed as a result of their membership.

The K-Rep requirements also influence the groups' choice of new members. Groups are increasingly reluctant to accept members unless they will be involved in the saving and lending activity, and some of the K-Rep officers encourage groups to reject members who do not participate in the lending programme. This means that the groups no longer include people who would previously have been members. These are mostly the poorer members who want to join the groups but are never really able to meet the financial requirements that are associated with membership. Regular savings, and even the traditional merry-go-rounds, involve financial commitments which the poorer members cannot meet.

K-Rep's Credit Officers also mentioned some other negative effects of collaboration. The leaders' workload naturally increases when the group takes a loan from K-Rep, and this may lead to problems, and it may even be related to the occasional cases of dishonesty which have already been mentioned. If a leader feels she is doing too much work for no reward, she may decide to take what she feels is owed to her without telling her colleagues. The regular meetings are also inconvenient for many of the members, who have extensive home and business responsibilities. This can lead to irregular attendance, which in turn contributes to poor savings and repayment performance.

The Impact of Outside Money—The Ekta Mahila Bachat Samuh

The Ekta Mahila Bachat Samuh group in Uttar Pradesh obtained an overdraft from the bank, and they also received a grant from a government department. The impact of this money was wholly positive. Attendance at meetings went up from 85% to 95%, and the members also agreed to increase their monthly savings from Rs. 10 to Rs. 30, because they were earning more, and they wanted to accumulate their own funds in order to borrow more in the future.

When they only had their own money to lend, 57% of the loans they took were for consumption. The outside money enabled them to borrow more for productive income-generating enterprises, so that the proportion of loans taken for consumption was reduced to 25%. The members have saved Rs. 3560, and they have also accumulated a surplus of Rs. 2818 from their on-lending operation. They owe Rs. 10000 to the bank, the full limit allowed. Their own funds thus amount to 39% of the total capital employed in their On-Lending Group.

Conclusion

It is difficult to come to any firm conclusions regarding the effects of outside money on the groups. The findings from Kenya in particular suggest that when groups focus their attention on finance, and on their relationship with an external lending institution, many of them cease to perform their social function. This may damage their ability to be effective financial intermediaries, but it can also be a result of their effort to become such intermediaries, and of their success in so doing.

The On-Lending Groups are going through a process of transformation from a social group with many mutually supporting activities, including a merry-go-round which is a form of saving and lending, but is also a powerful social "glue', into a micro-bank. This transformation can be interpreted as a classic example of progress and "development", wherein social and economic functions become separated and people form specialised and efficient institutions for particular tasks. Alternatively, it may be seen as the destruction of community solidarity, moving to a situation where people only remain within a group so long as it benefits them as individuals.

The situation in India is less stark, perhaps because Kenyans are more socially mobile than villagers in rural India, and because the Indian groups have more poor members than those in Kenya. It still has elements of the same transformation, however, and there does appear to be an almost inexorable process of 'trading up', whereby groups lose their weaker members and move up with the more successful, rather than losing those who outgrow them and taking new recruits from "below".

The reluctance of bankers in both countries to deal with potential "graduates" from On-Lending Groups on an individual basis contributes to this. People who have established an excellent track record as savers, and who have borrowed and successfully repaid a series of loans of increasing value, still find it impossible to make the transition and to become customers of a bank like any other, even if the same branch has been dealing with their group and is familiar with their record. Their only option is to stay with the group and to use their influence to make it offer the sort of services they need. This is profitable for the group in a financial sense, but the poorer members, who need more modest services and above all a social security "net", are inevitably marginalised and may have to leave.

It would be unrealistic to expect On-Lending Groups to be efficient financial intermediaries and at the same time be all-embracing community support organisations. Each has in any case to share some elements of the other, but undoubtedly the On-Lending Group is as equitable, as efficient, and as sympathetic an intermediary as is likely to exist. On-Lending Groups will certainly not solve all the problems of poverty, and they may make it even more necessary for NGOs to seek out the disadvantaged and to help them to form community groups which may in time evolve into On-Lending Groups.

CHAPTER 4

THE DEVELOPMENT AND ASSESSMENT OF ON-LENDING GROUPS

4.1. How can On-Lending Groups be Developed and Assessed?

Although commercial banks have only reached a very small proportion of the poorer people, particularly poorer women, many of these people are quite prepared to deal with a bank. There are large numbers of pre-existing groups, many of which are already involved in financial intermediation, and many individuals who have never had any dealings with a formal financial institution nevertheless have experience of regular saving.

This does not mean, however, that the On-Lending Group market is ready and waiting to do business with banks. Not every group needs or wants outside finance, even if they are fully qualified to make good use of it. Those groups which do need more funds than their own savings and accumulated surplus, also need to be informed, prepared and assessed before they can start to borrow. As with any new market segment, the supplier has to incur some marketing costs, in order to promote his products and educate the customers about the services which are available, and how to use them properly.

This On-Lending Group marketing function has thus far been mainly undertaken by NGOs, at no cost to the banks, although some banks in India have undertaken the task on their own, and K-Rep, functioning as a bank, has not generally taken up On-Lending Groups which have been in any way assisted by other NGOs. If the market is to be thoroughly exploited, however, the time and cost involved in the group promotion and assessment process must be examined.

Some information about this process is available, although much of the published material relates to the Grameen Bank Bangladesh type of groups, where less is demanded of the members. The AKRSP programme in the northern areas of Pakistan, for instance, developed quite slowly, and the Portu women's On-Lending Group did not get a loan from AKRSP until five years after it was formed. The Hussaini group only borrowed after nine years (Harper A, 1995, p.61). The group promotion process was also quite labour-intensive, and some individual women had to be visited in their homes "several times" (Bakhoum et al., 1989. pp.

8-9) before they would take, what was for them the quite daring step of joining a group.

In the Village Bank programme in Latin America and elsewhere, however, the promoter makes intensive visits for a one month "trial and training period", and thereafter the frequency of visits is drastically reduced (Holt, 1994, p.157). An earlier publication on the development of small farmer groups (Roberts and Harper (Eds.), 1980, p.43) recommended a promotion period of three to six months or longer.

Much of the experience relating to the promotion of On-Lending Groups for bank linkage relates to India. In addition to the current findings, some other organisations have also published information on this issue. Most NGOs are not under any pressure to reduce costs or achieve financial results by any particular time, and their field staff may be addressing a wide range of issues as well as financial intermediation when they are working with groups. The British DFID funded programmes in urban areas (Rutherford and Arora, 1997, p.22) found that NGOs normally keep visiting On-Lending Groups which they have promoted for "one or two years".

In Indore, however, under the same programme (ibid., p. 23) seventy On-Lending Groups were formed in one year. Within a year their savings had tripled, the cumulative loans which they had made from their own resources had more than tripled, and many of the groups had taken loans from the Indian affiliate of Friends of Women's World Banking, which acts in some respects like a bank.

NGOs which are themselves promoting, developing, assessing and financing On-Lending Groups, with the assistance of SIDBI or other development institutions, have found that the complete process can take between three months and two years (SIDBI, 1997). The poorer the members, the longer it takes.

PRADAN (PRADAN/NABARD, 1996, pp. 33-34) consider that the complete process of group formation takes up to two years. This starts with a two months pre-formation phase, when the idea is planted in the community. This is followed by four months of actual formation and six months of stabilisation, during which the group will start lending to its members from its accumulated savings.

During the following six months the group becomes further stabilised, and starts to pay an accountant to keep its records and forming clusters with other neighbouring groups. During the last six months of the two years , the NGO plays little or no role. The group may borrow from a bank during this period, and the clusters of groups will start the process of forming a federation, which may have several thousand members and which can itself perform the intermediation function between the clusters and their constituent groups, thus eliminating the need for any links with banks. At this point, the federation can also start to take over from the NGO the task of promoting new groups, so that the system becomes self-sustaining.

The National Bank for Agriculture and Rural Development (NABARD), which has initiated the programme of On-Lending or Self-Help Group linkage in India, and encourages the banks to participate with training and subsidised refinance, suggests in its guidelines that groups should have been saving regularly for at least six months before they are considered for bank loans. Some groups, how-ever, demand far more of themselves, and insist that they should have been saving for at least two years before they take a loan (NABARD, 1995, p.20).

The tasks of promoting On-Lending Groups, and of assessing their suitability for outside finance, are intimately linked. It is obviously important to ensure that the appraisal process is independent, and if a NGO puts forward a group as being ready to borrow money the banker will need to assess it himself. Similarly, if the lender is also the group promoter, some objective measures of acceptability will have to be imposed in order to avoid bias.

Bankers everywhere have attempted to design objective borrower appraisal methods, in order to simplify the process and to ensure consistency. It is never possible, however, to eliminate entirely the need for judgement of the human fac-tor, unless security is the only criterion. Groups are social entities, and it is neces-sary to judge not only the individual qualities of the On-Lending Group's mem-bers and particularly its officers, but also the social effectiveness of the group as a whole. The banker is effectively delegating much of the appraisal and recovery process to the group, and unless he is confident enough in the group to be willing to do this the advantages of group intermediation will be lost.

NGOs which are assisted by SIDBI have found that groups which demonstrate their own empowerment, in relations with government official or traders for in-stance, are also likely to be better financial intermediaries. Outside finance often enables On-Lending Groups to start lending for production rather than for con-sumption purposes, but groups which are already using some of their own savings for productive investments are also better candidates for loans than those which are only saving and lending for consumption. Groups which use their resources to create community assets also tend to be better intermediaries than those which focus entirely on the members' individual interests (SIDBI, 1997).

Because On-Lending Group intermediation demands a new and unfamiliar approach to loan appraisal, there have been a number of attempts to assist lenders in the appraisal process. The original NABARD guidelines (PRADAN, 1996, p.1) suggested in 1991 that an On-Lending Group should have been in existence for at least six months and should have been saving regularly for that period. These guidelines are purely indicative, since NABARD's role is only to promote group lending with subsidised refinance and training; the lending banks take all the risk, and are thus free to decide for themselves to which groups they should lend, if any.

A year later, in 1992, NABARD added further guidelines. They suggested that self-help groups should also have some successful experience in lending to their members from the group's resources, they should be keeping records, they should be homogeneous and democratic, they should not be lead by local political leaders and the members should want to borrow for individual rather than group-based enterprises.

MYRADA (Fernandes, 1992, p.63) suggested that banks should demand more. They should ensure that at least three quarters of the members regularly attended meetings, that loans were evenly distributed among the membership, that the of-ficers were changed regularly and that the group was willing to apply sanctions to defaulting members when necessary. They also stress the importance of treating the group as the customer, rather than its individual members. MYRADA is presumably confident in its own ability to assess groups, but they nevertheless insist that bankers should satisfy themselves that a group is creditworthy. They suggest that the banker should visit each group at least two or preferably three times himself, rather than relying entirely on the NGO's judgement.

The bankers in Orissa followed the NABARD assessment guidelines, as supplemented in some cases by their own banks, but they also stressed the particular importance of assessing the group's savings history. They enquired about members' earlier experience of traditional saving in kind, such as with rice banks, and they also examined the trend of members' savings over time. Initial enthusiasm may be followed by apathy, and they felt that On-Lending Groups must be able to show that all members had saved regularly, with increasing or at least the same amounts.

In some cases members of groups in Orissa were unaware of the financial position of the group as a whole, or even of their own savings balance. Bankers and NGOs suggested that one effective way of assessing the quality of group leadership and member participation was to ask members what their savings balance was. If they did not know, this was a bad sign.

The bankers in Maharashtra, Karnataka and Uttar Pradesh felt that the quality of an On-Lending Group could be judged from the regularity of its meetings, savings and repayment of loans, besides the involvement of leaders and participation of its members.

It was felt to be essential that groups should have regular meetings, as the members had decided while formulating their bye-laws. Regular meetings maintained the discipline of the group members, and as the meetings were also used for collecting savings and loan repayments, this gave the members a clear target for when they had to have saved a specific amount of money. The groups promoted by Cauvery Grameena Bank, Canara Bank, Oriental Bank of Commerce, IYD and MYRADA held weekly meetings, whereas the groups promoted by other agencies held fortnightly or monthly meetings.

The frequency of meetings was not important; what mattered was their regularity and punctuality. The members of On-Lending Groups which met at weekly intervals felt that such frequent meetings helped because the amount of their savings and loan repayments were small. Frequent meetings also helped in other non-financial activities, such as, literacy promotion.

Out of the 52 groups which were studied only six groups had missed even as many as one or two meetings during the year 1996/97, and all the 19 groups in Orissa were said to conduct their meetings regularly at the scheduled times. None of the 14 groups which were studied in Uttar Pradesh had cancelled even one meeting during the year. The members of all the groups, including those which met weekly, said they had no difficulty in attending them. The women members in particular looked forward to the meetings as social occasions.

Table 14 summarises the meeting attendance record of the On-Lending Groups that were studied in Karnataka, Maharashtra and Uttar Pradesh.

Table 14: Details of Attendance at Meetings for 1996-97

State	Promoted by	Total no. of On-Lending Groups	Number of groups in different attendance ranges		
			> 80%	60%-80%	< 60%
Karnataka	NGO	12	2	7	3
	Bank	13	9	4	-
Maharashtra	NGO	10	7	3	-
Uttar Pradesh	NGO	6	5	1	-
	Bank	8	6	1	1
Total		49	29	16	4

The three NGO-promoted On-Lending Groups in Karnataka had been given grants for group irrigation projects early in their existence, and this led to their being dominated by a few members and their subsequent collapse.

There was some decline in the regularity of attendance in some of the older On-Lending Groups. The eight groups in Karnataka which were more than five years old all suffered a decline in attendance. Three of these were men's groups promoted by MYRADA which are now defunct, but there was also some decline in the remaining five, which were women's groups. In these cases, attendance dropped from about 98% initially to 61%. The MYRADA representatives said that this was because the members were not able to identify and pursue any profitable economic activities, although they had functioned as an On-Lending Group for more than five years.

Regular attendance was closely associated with good repayment, both within the On-Lending Groups and from the groups to the banks, which confirms that this is a reliable assessment measure.

On-Lending Group intermediation is of recent origin, and as bankers gather more experience they will no doubt evolve more effective and possibly less subjective techniques for assessment. At this stage, however, the bankers who were interviewed in this study were more or less in agreement that that following are the critical factors which need to be examined while assessing On-Lending Groups:

Felt need for group formation
The group members must have come together with a genuine sense of self-help, and a shared felt need to form the group. Groups which come together only to get bank loans tend to disintegrate sooner or later.

Homogeneity
On-Lending Groups should be homogeneous in terms of caste, economic status, age and sex, or a common interest may be sufficient. In general, the more homogenous a group is, the better are its chances of success.

Financial operations
The savings and credit operations must be carefully appraised. This includes the regularity and amount of savings and the way the group ensures that this is

maintained, their systems of loan appraisal and prioritising loans, their repayment systems and the mechanisms developed by the group to deal with defaults.

Discipline and awareness

On-Lending Groups must have basic rules and the members should be aware of and adhere to them. Regularity in savings, loan repayments, meetings, and attendance are indicators of group discipline.

Leadership and democracy

The way in which leaders are selected and the positions are rotated, and the ways in which they make decisions are essential indicators of an effective On-Lending Group.

Systems and procedures

On-Lending Groups must have clear systems and procedures and officers must be clearly accountable. This applies particularly to the handling of cash and bank accounts and loan sanctioning.

Independence

The extent to which the On-Lending Group is dependent on its original pro-moter or on a few of its members has to be assessed. The group must be moving towards independence, even if it has not yet been achieved.

Basix Finance, a recently established rural financial institution, which operates in Karnataka and Andhra Pradesh, is experimenting with an On-Lending Group rating system. This attempts to combine qualitative and quantitative assess-ment, and to come up with a score on which the decision to lend, and the multiple of the groups' savings to be lent if the decision is positive, can be based. This is still being developed, and it is too early to confirm its value, but it does represent an interesting innovation in that Basix is not bound by any externally imposed conditions, such as are required by banks which take advantage of subsidised refi-nance from NABARD, and Basix is a financial institution, albeit one with a social mandate, and has not evolved from an NGO.

The questionnaire includes questions about the following aspects of the group which is a prospective borrower:

- Age and the reasons why the group was started
- Members, their number and social homogeneity, and their wealth (with higher marks being awarded for poorer members)
- Governance and independence from other organisations or influence
- Record-keeping, and the regularity, attendance and frequency of meetings
- Savings (including a simple formula to check whether the total accumulated is consistent with the stated age of the group, and the frequency and amounts of savings)
- The way in which lending decisions are made
- The interest rates the group charges (with higher marks for higher rates, and

the highest for rates which depend on the purpose of the loans)
- Recovery performance, and the impact on members
- Accumulated reserves.

The groups are marked out of a total of 700 points; 270 of these are awarded for internal financial performance, with less weighting being given to social factors, governance and external relationships. Basix plans to introduce this group grading system together with a performance-related scheme to reimburse NGOs or other for the costs of promoting groups which become eligible for loans.

K-Rep's Assessment Process

K-Rep has studied and documented the process of On-Lending Group assessment in some detail (Mwaniki et al., 1993; Mutua et al., 1996). Our study found that the K-Rep credit officers do follow these guidelines, but they also add their own extra indicators depending on local conditions. This is correct, because each group has its own peculiar characteristics and all can not be judged on an equal basis.

K-Rep's own guidelines state that the On-Lending Group must:
- be in the specified area of the particular K-Rep Office
- have members who are currently running small or micro-enterprises
- be registered with the relevant Government authorities
- be registered with K-Rep
- have an account for depositing members savings
- demonstrate capacity to administer loan funds
- demonstrate unity among the members
- have been operating a merry-go-round for at least one year
- show that its members' businesses have been in existence for at least one year.

The assessment criteria do not stop at the group level but they also include the individual members. K-Rep states that the individual members of the group must:
- be 18 years of age or more
- be Kenyan citizens
- not be close family relatives of other group members
- own and operate a business within the area
- be willing to abide by the rules laid down in the group constitution
- attend all weekly/monthly group meetings
- show a commitment to abide by all K-Rep policies and procedures

The K-Rep Credit Officers have also themselves adopted various other indicators to assess whether a On-Lending Group will be a good intermediary, on the basis of their own experience. They include the following:

Credit Officers (CO)	Other indicators
CO 1	business turnover of members commitment of the individual to the group
CO 2	commitment to savings mobilisation strong group leadership
CO 3	group cohesion group activities regular group meetings involvement of all members in the group activities
CO 4	types of business run by members business turnovers participation in group activities
CO 5	stability of the group volume of savings mobilised members' business turnover
CO 6	leadership of the group character of the group members participation in group activities volume of savings mobilised by the group
CO 7	unity in the group type of businesses operated by the members
CO 8	strong leadership group activities
CO 9	conduct of the group members maintenance of group records active participation of members in group activities group activities
CO 10	strong leadership how members relate to one another character of individual members group activities

Many of these indicators are subjective, and are closely related to the more "official" list which was given above. One item that is frequently mentioned by the Credit Officers, however, is the importance of group activities and members' participation in them. This suggests that their experience has shown that groups which become too focused on purely financial functions may in fact become less reliable financial intermediaries than those which retain some of their more traditional social functions.

Every K-Rep Credit Officer applies some combination of the "official" indicators and his or her own ideas, but the six core points which are used to assess the eligibility of an On-Lending Group for a loan can be summarised as follows:

- The group must be registered with the Government authorities and K-Rep
- It must prove that it has been in existence and operated a merry-go-round for at least one year
- It must have or agree to open a savings account for members' savings
- It must have a well-formulated working constitution
- It must conduct regular disciplined group meetings with full participation
- The members must all have individual businesses nearby.

Other Kenyan microfinance institutions, apart from K-Rep, were agreed as a result of their experience in dealing with On-Lending Groups that certain indicators are critical to determining that a group can be a good intermediary. These may usefully be summarised in the form of questions:

Leadership: Is the leader active without dominating the group's activities ? Does she involve all the members in the group activities without dominating them, and can she manage internal conflicts smoothly ?

Discipline: Is the group well-disciplined ? Are meetings punctual and well-attended ?

Participation: Do all the members save regularly and to the right amount? Do they all participate in all the group's activities ?

Honesty: Do the group officers and members frankly and openly talk about its past history ? Do they give accurate figures of their past savings ?

Organisation: Is the group well organised ? Are the books up-to-date ?

Commitment: Does the group consistently conform to the lender's requirements ?

The Development of On-Lending Groups – The Tumaini Group

Mrs. Agnes Nzua started the Tumaini group in Machakos, Kenya, in 1992. She started with seven friends, and they then persuaded 32 other women to join them. Their objective was to organise a merry-go-round in order to raise capital for business and personal use. They had also heard that various NGOs were willing to help businesswomen like themselves, if they were organised in groups. They were registered in 1993; eight members dropped out shortly thereafter, because they were not willing to adhere to the new rules requiring regular attendance at meetings and savings.

The Tumaini group heard about K-Rep in 1995, and they asked if they could join the programme. The K-Rep credit officer visited them about eight times, for about an hour each time, and she eventually concluded that they should be accepted. They had been in existence for almost three years, they were officially registered, they had a group savings account, and they had savings equal to 10% of the amount they wished to borrow.

Several members had difficulty repaying the loans they had taken from the first loan which the group received from K-Rep, but eventually they all repaid. As a result of this experience, nine members left one other member died, and seven others also left for a variety of reasons. One moved her business too far away for the group to be confident that she would repay regularly in future, a thief stole all the stocks of another member, so that she had to close her business down, and two others were close relatives; the other members, and K-Rep, felt that this might lead to difficulties if one went into arrears. One member opted out of the merry-go-round and was expelled, and two others had formal jobs, which was not permitted under K-Rep's rules.

In spite of these difficulties, The Tumaini group repaid its first loan to K-Rep, and they then took a second loan. Two of the members chose not to borrow from this. The other 12 members are all repaying on time, and have reduced the outstanding amount to Kshs. 629,000 (about US$12000). All the members continue to save Kshs. 200 every month, and they also have a number of different merry-go-rounds, to which they contribute between one and five thousand shillings each month.

The Tumaini group has experienced a number of problems since it was started. The founder herself borrowed the group's funds for a brief period for her own use without asking her fellow-members, but she returned the whole amount when she was discovered, and has remained a member. In spite of these problems, however, the group has remained an excellent customer for K-Rep.

Conclusion

Although the use of On-Lending Groups for financial intermediation is quite new, there is a reasonable body of knowledge about group development in general, and the foregoing suggests that the criteria for judging whether a group is effective are little different from those used for any other form of group assessment. The criteria are, however, very different from those with which bankers are familiar.

The judgement of the On-Lending Group as a social entity must also of course be supplemented by a judgement of its financial strength and record. This is in some ways simpler for a banker than judging any other type of business, because he should know how to judge a bank. He need not know about the details of the particular enterprises the members are engaged in. Their local knowledge and personal familiarity with their fellow-members, and the fact that their own money is at risk if anyone fails, mean that they are far more qualified than any outsider to judge the feasibility of their businesses.

If the group can show a track record of saving, lending and recovery, and if its members' savings, which are effectively their equity investment in their own micro-bank, conform to whatever standards the lending institution has chosen, this should be enough.

The process of assessment is not simple, but the Indian Bank Managers who had long experience of traditional lending were all agreed that assessment of an On-Lending Group was easier and quicker than assessing a similar direct lending proposal. The Canara Bank, Ittanahalli branch manager compared an On-Lending Group loan proposal for Rs. 50,000 (US$1430) with an individual proposal for a borewell and pumpset costing the same amount. He explained that in the case of the direct loan he had to obtain and verify 8 to 10 documents such as land records, groundwater availability certificate, a quotation from the driller and the pumpset dealer, a feasibility certificate from the State Electricity Board and so on. In the case of a loan to a group for the same amount, the branch manager had only to attend one or two meetings of the group, to interact with the members and to form an opinion. Further, because the ultimate uses of the loan to the On-Lending Group were not his concern, the manager was saved the trouble of ensuring utilisation, periodical inspection of assets, and so on.

4.2. What Does It Cost to Develop and to Assess an On-Lending Group ?

There have been various estimates of the cost of forming an On-Lending Group. Most commentators are agreed that the costs, both for the bank and the group member, are lower than if the bank was dealing direct with the individual, although this is a somewhat theoretical comparison because most banks do not deal direct with this type of customer, unless it is in the context of a subsidised scheme where the cost is immaterial. Pulhazendi (1995), for instance, calculated that in southern India the bank's transaction costs per individual client were reduced by 40%, while the borrower's costs, assuming that she could get a loan at all, were 85% lower than if she had had to borrow individually from the bank.

One report (SPARC, 1995, p.11) quotes a group development cost of Rs. 7360, or approximately $210, over three years, and this is remarkably consistent with the approximate range of between Rs. 5000 and Rs. 10000 which it was suggested was the cost for the SIDBI financed NGOs which were engaged in microfinance (SIDBI, 1997). Another paper (Krishnamurthy, 1992, pp. 4-5) mentions a figure of Rs. 180 per member;. If the average On-Lending Group has twenty members, this amounts to about $100 for a whole group, or half the earlier cost, but it is said not to include the animators' salary cost; if this is added, the total cost might be quite similar.

MYRADA, the Indian agency which has perhaps the longest documented experience of working with On-Lending Groups, has calculated a rather higher figure of $530. In addition to $ 170 for members training, $10 for account books, $100 for the MYRADA staff costs and $75 allowance for the group leader, this total includes a $ 175 grant of 'seed money' which has since been discontinued; the balance of $355 is still well over the other figures (Foundation for Development Cooperation, 1992, p.214). The leaders of most On-Lending Groups seem willing to act without any allowance. If the leader's allowance is eliminated, the balance is similar to the $200 figure quoted above.

Very few NGOs keep a separate record of the cost of promoting On-Lending Groups, since this is only one component of their development work and the staff who are engaged on it also do other work in the same communities.

Fellowship is an NGO which has promoted 75 groups in Bhadrak in northern Orissa, of which 40 have received bank finance. They estimate that the variable cost of promoting one On-Lending Group is Rs. 250, or $7. This covers stationery, passbooks and staff travel. The total of the other costs is about Rs. 130,000 per year. Some part of this amount is spent on maintaining contact with older groups, but the majority is spent on promoting newer ones. In 1996-97, 23 new groups were formed; if it is assumed that the entire amount was spent on new groups, the cost per group, including the variable cost, would be about $170, which is again not dissimilar to the other figures quoted above. MASS in Sambalpur, also in Orissa, reports an average promotion cost of about $140 per group.

NGO costs are notoriously difficult to assess, since their activities are generally integrated, and many of their operating costs are subsidised by grants, by gifts in kind and by the contributions of their clients. Their staff may also work for negligible wages. SOPORTE, a small NGO which also operates near Bhadrak, has two staff members dedicated to On-Lending Group promotion, but the wages, allowances and other expenses for both of them amount only to about $450 per year. SOPORTE has promoted a total of 30 groups in two years, which means that the cost of promoting each group is only $30.

These very low costs are clearly not directly comparable with those of a bank, with higher paid professional staff for whom group promotion is not directly related to their other work. The Manager of the Pingua branch of Dhenkenal Rural Bank in Orissa, which has been a leader in the State in the promotion of On-Lending-Groups without any help from NGOs, estimated that he had to spend about 28 hours with each group before it was ready to take a loan, while his field officer would have to spend about 72 hours. The total cost, including overheads, would be about Rs. 5000, or $140, but if the cost of training the group's officers to keep the necessary simple records was included, the cost came to about Rs. 7000, or $200.

In order to compare the cost of promoting an On-Lending Group by a NGO with that of a bank, a detailed study was made of the respective costs incurred by the New Public School Samiti (NPSS), an NGO, and one branch of the Aligarh Grameen Bank, both operating in similar places in Uttar Pradesh.

The time taken by different employees of the NGO at different stages of group formation was estimated to be as shown in Table 15.

Table 15: Time and Cost of Group Development by NPSS

Year One Activity	Co-ordinator	Accountant	Field Worker	Total hours	Approx. Cost
Survey	2 hours	1 hour	4 hours	7 hours	
Formation	2 hours	1 hour	24 hours (6 visits)	27 hours	
Monitoring	4 hours	8 hours	28 hours (7 visits)	40 hours	
Liaison with bank			12 hours (12 visits)	12 hours	
Total	8 hours	10 hours	68 hours	86 hours	Rs. 2700
Year Two	6 hours	12 hours	48 hours	66 hours	Rs. 2250
Year Three	6 hours	12 hours	48 hours	66 hours	Rs. 2250
Year Four	4 hours	12 hours	16 hours	32 hours	Rs. 650
Year Five	2 hours	12 hours	8 hours	22 hours	Rs. 450
Year Six		12 hours		12 hours	Rs. 220

The time spent in years two to six is for a combination of monitoring, liaison with the bank and generally maintaining contact. From year four onwards, the amount of contact is substantially reduced. The staff costs per hour are based on an effective 150-hour working month, and they include salaries, overheads and allowances, as well as the cost of training the staff for this work and of the books and stationery that are given to the groups. They allow for the gradual reduction in the length and frequency of the NGO workers' visits over the period, and the decreasing need for liaison visits to the bank on behalf of the group. These figures are based on the time taken to develop the first On-Lending Groups which NPSS promoted.

The NGO estimates that the costs will be reduced by about a third or more for later groups, as a result of improved staff performance and the members' own learning from their neighbours' experiences. The village surveys and the Coordinator's meetings with village elders are not needed for later groups. One visit by a man and a woman field worker are adequate for this purpose. The District Coordinator still visits once in four months, and a field worker visits once a month. Additional visits by the field worker may also be required during the process of establishing the group's relationship with the bank. After an On-Lending Group has been successfully launched in a particular village, it naturally arouses the curiosity and interest of other people in that village. At that stage if any effort is made to form another group of those who were not included in the first group, it can be developed with much less effort.

The total expenditure on the On-Lending Group by the NGO in the first three years is thus Rs. 7200 or about $200. Thereafter, the cost is very significantly reduced. Although the primary purpose of promoting the groups was to enable them to become sustainable On-Lending Groups, the NPSS staff inevitably carried out other community development tasks when they were working with the groups. It is not possible totally to isolate the costs of group development.

Most of the On-Lending Groups which were promoted by banks in the area covered by this study were promoted by Regional Rural Banks. This was because the chairmen of the particular banks had decided to promote group linkages vigorously, regardless of whether there were effective NGOs to promote them in the branch's areas or not. In the case of Canara Bank in Karnataka, On-Lending Groups were also formed by the branch managers on their own initiative. For the purpose of estimating the cost of group promotion by a bank, the experience of the Narauna branch of Aligarh Grameen Bank in Uttar Pradesh was analysed in some detail.

The branch manager worked through the network of the farmers' club in his area in order to form On-Lending Groups. The manager already knew most of the members of the club, but it took some time to convince them about the efficacy of On-Lending Groups. He visited the village ten times over a period of six months and interacted with the club members intensively. Even after formation of the groups, he felt that they required close monitoring and decided that he would visit them once a month for the next three years.

Table 16 gives comparative figures worked out for the Aligarh Grameen Bank based on their salary levels and the number of visits they made, and estimated they would make, to the groups they developed.

Table 16: Time and Cost of Group Development by Aligarh Grameen Bank, Narauna Branch

Year One Activity	Manager	Clerk	Field worker	Total hours	Approx. cost
Survey	8 hours (4 visits)		6 hours (3 visits)	14 hours	
Formation	22 hours (11 visits)		24 hours (12 visits)	46 hours	
Monitoring	3 hours		3 hours	6 hours	
Records	3 hours	6 hours	3 hours	12 hours	
Total	36 hours	6 hours	36 hours	78 hours	Rs. 5000
Year Two	9 hours	6 hours	9 hours	24 hours	Rs. 1500
Year Three	9 hours	6 hours	9 hours	24 hours	Rs. 1500
Year Four	7 hours	6 hours	7 hours	20 hours	Rs. 1300
Year Five	5 hours	6 hours	5 hours	16 hours	Rs. 1000
Year Six	3 hours	6 hours	3 hours	12 hours	Rs. 700

Many of these costs were similar to those incurred with any customer of a similar scale. It is unlikely, however, that any manager would make as many visits to a conventional customer as the Narauna branch manager did to these groups; he was willing to do this because he was anxious himself to be familiar with this new type of business, so that he could in future encourage and assist his staff to develop more groups. He was also encouraged in this work by the enthusiasm of the Chairman of the Bank.

The manager estimated that the groups which his branch was now developing, after their initial satisfactory experience, would cost less than half as much to develop; the initial formation process in particular would be much quicker, and he would be able to entrust most of this work to his field officers.

This shows that the Bank's first year cost of formation and nurturing an On-Lending Group was Rs. 5,000, or about $140, and was thus more than twice the cost of the NGO's first year. The Bank's cost declined steeply in the subsequent two years, however, giving a three-year total of about Rs 8000, which is very similar to the NGO figure. It is also not dissimilar close to the figure of $200 for the Pingua branch of Dhenkenal Rural Bank in Orissa.

The Bank's branch manager and field officer found that it was no longer necessary to meet members regularly, or to attend the group meetings, after the first year. This was mainly because the groups formed by the banks were of comparatively better-off members who could manage the group's affairs on their own. The manager was also able to combine later visits to the groups with his routine village visits.

The comparative costs for the NGO and the Bank of the initial year of group formation, and of the subsequent monitoring process, are as follows:

Table 17. India. Comparative Cost of Group Formation by NGO (NPSS) and Bank
(Aligarh Grameen Bank)

Promoting agency	Cost of group formation (1st year)	Cost of group development (years 2-3)	Cost of group monitoring (years 4-6)	Total cost
NGO	Rs. 2700	Rs. 4500	Rs. 1320	Rs. 8520
Bank	Rs. 5000	Rs. 3000	Rs. 3000	Rs. 11000

The Bank estimated that its staff would spend a total of 174 hours during the six years, whereas the NGO estimated 284 hours. The average cost per hour of bank staff was about Rs. 63, or just under US$2, whereas the cost of NGO staff was less than half this amount, Rs. 30 or about 85 cents. This difference was in part absorbed by the fact that the bank staff focused their attention solely on the development of the groups' ability to become viable on-lending customers, whereas the NGO staff were inevitably also concerned with other aspects of community development.

The Bank's high costs in the first year were mainly the result of the manager's insistence that he should personally be involved at every stage. In subsequent years, the bank's cost of developing and monitoring the groups was reduced, because the NGO officials made more frequent visits. The bankers may also have been able to give the groups a firmer initial grounding in the necessary simple financial management and recording skills. The Bank manager was also able to take advantage of his routine visits to the village to attend the group meetings.

These figures show that on present performance, NGOs are less expensive agencies for promoting On-Lending Groups than banks, but not by a very wide margin. If banks appreciate the profit potential of this new approach to intermediation, they may be expected to identify more efficient ways of promoting groups. There are a number of ways in which this may be possible, since On-Lending Group development has not so far been recognised as a specialist function in its own right, but is a byproduct of general community development or other welfare work.

One Indian rural bank is planning to undertake an experiment whereby a selected branch would recruit five reasonably well-educated young women as specialist group developers. They would each be expected to develop about 25 groups a year, and the total cost per group, including supervision and overheads, is estimated to be well under fifty dollars.

Basix Finance is also discussing a performance-based On-Lending Group development scheme with a number of NGOs in Khammam District of eastern Andhra Pradesh. The details of this have yet to be finalised, but it is envisaged that the carefully selected participating NGOs would initially be paid a flat service charge for each group they brought to a satisfactory level of development, and would thereafter receive a commission on the interest earned on loans made to the groups. They would also be paid a service charge for two years after the first loan, to cover the cost of continuing assistance. The actual amounts are not yet finalised, but the total fee would almost certainly be well under the prototype costs incurred by NPSS and the Aligarh Grameen Bank.

The cost of assessment

Although On-Lending Group development and assessment are two different tasks, it is difficult to separate their costs when both are carried out by the same institution. The above figures compared the costs of carrying out this complete process. It is in fact quite rare for banks themselves to do this; they normally depend on NGOs to develop the groups and to recommend them for financing. At this point, the banker has only to ascertain whether the group is indeed bankable, and not to make it so.

The use of On-Lending Groups for intermediation clearly does not totally absolve the lender from the normal process of prudent appraisal. MYRADA (Fernandes, 1992, p.29) suggests that the branch manager must visit the group at least three times in order to assess members' needs, and PRADAN recommends (PRADAN/NABARD, 1996, p.40) that he should attend at least two meetings of the group before making his decision. SIDBI (1997) suggest that the NGOs which they finance have to spend about 10% of the amount of their first loan to On-Lending Groups on their assessment; the average first loan is about Rs. 10,000, which means that their assessment cost is one thousand rupees, or about thirty dollars.

Experience in South Africa, on the other hand (Cashbank, 1993), has apparently led one banker to conclude that the only effective way to appraise a group is to do business with them in a small way, starting with savings mobilisation and proceeding gradually to very small, very short-term loans; in her opinion, the only way to learn was by doing.

The transaction costs also include post-disbursement monitoring and supervision. MYRADA suggest (NABARD, 1995, p.35) that the promoting NGO should only withdraw after the On-Lending Group has accumulated four to five years of successful experience, and if no NGO has been involved the banker must presumably maintain a similar level of contact. Fong and Perrett (1991, p.141) state that there is a need for "constant supervision and support" by the formal financial institution. Most of the limited data that have been reported on the cost of assessing On-Lending Group loans relate to comparisons with direct loans rather than the absolute figures.

The Rastriya Banijya Bank of Nepal, for instance, reported a 47% saving in transaction costs when lending through On-Lending Groups (Foundation for Development Cooperation, 1992, p.42), and a rapid study in Karnataka showed a 38% saving (NABARD, 1995, p.31). The bankers in Orissa who responded to a 1996 survey by NABARD in Orissa (Panda and Mishra, 1996, pp. 41-42) were all agreed that appraisal of loans to On-Lending Groups took less time than other loans, although the times they gave differed very much from one bank to another. One Regional Rural Bank reported that it took a total of two days work to appraise and process one loan, which cost Rs. 600 salary plus overheads. Canara Bank reported that appraisal required five days, or forty hours, which cost Rs. 1500, and other banks said that it took 20 hours.

Indian banks, reporting on their experience of appraising groups which had been promoted by MYRADA (Foundation for Development Cooperation, 1992, p.114), reported that the cost of making individual loans to similar small borrowers was Rs. 157 per borrower, whereas it was reduced to Rs. 103 when the borrowers were members of On-Lending Groups. In general, there was a 50% saving in transaction costs, irrespective of the improvement in recovery. This saving was in spite of the fact that the bank still had a separate record for each borrower, and was not at this time really treating the group as a single borrower. Hatton National Bank in Sri Lanka reported (ibid., p.192) that their transaction costs for an On-Lending Group loan were as low as 3.3% of the value of the loan.

The same publication from which many of the above findings are taken, however, concludes (ibid., p.50) that the On-Lending Group transaction costs of banks and of NGOs are not really known, and that further research is needed, particularly on the apportionment of costs within NGOs, and between them and the banks. This issue is addressed in this study.

The detailed costs of appraising an On-Lending Group which had been promoted by a NGO were studied in a branch of the Kolar District Regional Rural Bank, in Karnataka, which has extensive experience of working with groups in collaboration with MYRADA and other NGOs such as AKAY, who were involved in this case (Table 18). The Bank insisted that the groups should be subjected to rigorous analysis, and the manager also had a detailed checklist of the characteristics a group should have before it was accepted for financing.

The branch manager was in constant touch with the NGO and relied heavily on their judgement regarding the strength of the groups. He also undertook a pre-sanction visit to the groups to interact with the members and scrutinise their registers. He paid special attention to the details of the transactions in their savings bank accounts, the regularity of their savings and the repayment record of loans they had made from their own funds.

Table 18. Kolar Rural Bank; Cost of Assessing an On-Lending Group
Promoted by a NGO

Item of assessment	Time taken	
	Clerk	Branch manager/ field officer
Identification of the group	-	2 hours
Pre-sanction visit	-	2 hours
Application/document verification etc.	½ hour	¼ hour
Loan appraisal sanction and disbursement	1 hour	1 hour
Post-sanction visit	-	2 hours
Follow-up and recovery	¾ hours	1 hour
Total	2¼ hours	8¼ hours
Approximate per hour cost	Rs. 45	Rs. 65
Cost of time spent	Rs. 100	Rs. 540
Total	Rs. 640	

The average loan from the branch to each group was Rs.9,212. The cost of assessment was therefore 7% of the loan disbursed by the branch to the group.

This is similar to the figure of 10% of the initial loan which was said by Indian microfinance NGOs to be their cost of assessment.

K-Rep's Costs of Group Promotion

When an On-Lending Group approaches K-Rep, the first thing the credit officer does is to meet the group. After two meetings, the credit officer decides whether to proceed with further meetings with the group or not. This decision is based on the members' regularity in attendance at meetings and the officer' impression of the group's overall management and initiative. The credit officer then spends one month introducing the group to K-Rep and explaining the lending procedures. After this period, the group can qualify for registration with K-Rep. After registration, the group has to save either on a weekly or a monthly basis to raise the required 10% of the loan.

The findings show that on average, a credit officer makes seven visits to a group during this process in order to assess it. Each visit lasts on an average for one hour and 40 minutes, which amounts in total to between 11 and 12 hours.

Table 19: Kenya. Average number of visits and time taken to assess an On-Lending Group

Variable	Mean	Minimum	Maximum
No. of visits	8.11	5	14
Time per visit	1.55	1.00	2.00
Transport costs (in Kshs.)	260.00	40	480
Credit Officer's salary cost (in Kshs.)	981.00	479.05	1768.80
Other costs (in Kshs.)	100.00	0	100
Total costs (in Kshs.)	1127.70	579.05	2008.80

The following table gives the costs incurred in assessing the groups which were the subject of detailed study:

Table 20: Kenya. Costs of Assessing On-Lending Groups

Groups/ costs	No. of visits	Time per visit (hours)	Transport costs (Kshs.)	Other costs (Kshs.)	Credit Officers' salary for time spent (Kshs.)	Total expenses (Kshs.)
Kaaga	12	2	240	0	2880	3120
Kyeni	5	2	400	0	1200	1600
Marigu	8	2	480	0	1200	1680
Mitumba	14	1.30	0	0	2520	2520
Tumaini	8	1	0	0	960	960
Wanyua	6	2	250	100	1440	1790
Wihoke	5	1.30	150	0	900	1050
Zaburi	8	2	0	0	1920	1920
Kerugoya	7	1.30	40	0	1260	1300

In arriving at the proportion of the salary based on the hours the credit officers stay with each group per visit, the average monthly salary of a credit officer (Kshs. 17,685, or about US$320) is divided into an effective working day of six hours, for 25 days a month. This gives a cost per hour of approximately Kshs. 120 or US$2.20.

The table above shows a breakdown of the expenses and costs incurred by K-Rep staff in assessing the groups that were used in this study. The credit officers' salary cost is clearly the major item. When the costs are added together, K-Rep spends approximately Kshs. 1770 (US$ 32) to assess one group. K-Rep's audited accounts for the year ending 1996 include office expenses, or overheads, of Kshs. 5,769,692, or about US$ 105,000. If this figure is divided by the total number of 778 groups with which the branches were dealing at the end of 1996, the average overhead cost per group comes to about US$135 per group. If we add that to the above figure of US$32, the total cost of dealing with one group comes to about $167. This is quite similar to the Indian figures, although it must be remembered that the Kenyan groups come to K-Rep as existing groups, and not as individuals to many of whom the whole concept of group financial intermediation must be introduced from the very beginning.

K-Rep officers stated that on an average, it takes three months to assess a group. Representatives from other microfinance institutions also stated that their assessment takes between one and three months. Kenya Women Finance Trust (KWFT) take approximately one-and-a-half months to assess a group. Though they do not provide training to the members, they orient them on the principles of KWFT credit delivery. The group leaders are given more specialised training.

It takes CARE Kenya approximately three months to assess a group. The assessment period includes training for the Revolving Loan Fund (RLF) leaders. During that period the leaders are introduced to revolving loan fund and business management. CARE Kenya spends Kshs. 9,000 (US$ 160) on training alone for each group, in addition to transport, follow-up and other credit operation costs.

Faulu Kenya were of the opinion that the time taken in assessing a group depends upon its level of maturity. If a group is mature and serious in its activities, assessment takes on an average two months. Younger and less organised groups may take as long as three months. Faulu do not provide any training to the group except orientation about the loan process, and they have never attempted to estimate the cost of preparing a group for intermediation.

The findings are consistent with those of Mutua et al. (1996), who in their study of the history of group based credit programmes in Kenya found that on an average, a group requires at least three months of preparation before it can apply for a loan.

Conclusion

The above analysis of the costs of developing and assessing On-Lending Groups included the following figures per group:

NABARD report	$ 200
MYRADA	$ 280
Fellowship	$ 140
SOPORTE	$ 30
NPSS	$ 200
Dhenkenal Rural Bank	$ 200
Aligarh Grameen Bank	$ 225
K-Rep	$ 170

The figures are fairly consistent with one another, in spite of being drawn from very different types of organisations, in different countries. The tasks were by no means identical, ranging from the introduction of the very concept of group intermediation, to people with little experience of working together in any way, to the assessment of a group which is already a micro-bank in its own right, saving and lending from its own resources.

Nevertheless, it does not appear unreasonable to conclude that the cost of developing a retail outlet which will reach around 20 new customers, with a limited but expanding borrowing capacity, is around two hundred dollars. Bankers should be able to judge for themselves whether this represents value for money.

4.3. Should the Bank or the NGO Develop On-Lending Groups?

We are attempting to show that ordinary bank branches can do business with On-Lending Groups without having to set up special departments or to undertake any functions which are fundamentally different from what they are accustomed to. Community group development is certainly not an activity which banks regularly undertake as part of their normal course of business, and we should not like to suggest that intermediation through groups depends on their doing this. Many bankers in India have of course promoted On-Lending Groups themselves, without any help from a NGO, and some 24 such groups, together with the banks which promoted them, are included in this study. It would probably be unreasonable to expect this to become general practice, however, since the task demands particular skills and attitudes, and a heavy commitment of out-of-office time.

Our cost data suggest that it is in any case less expensive for groups to be developed by NGOs than by banks, and there is some other evidence which supports this not very surprising finding. An international conference of bankers and NGO representatives on the subject of On-Lending Group intermediation were agreed that banks should leave the group development task to NGOs (NABARD-APRACA, 1996, p.93), and it was found in the SANASA movement in Sri Lanka that staff of the Federation of societies, many of whom often volunteers, were both cheaper and more effective than the lending bank's own staff (Foundation for Development Cooperation, 1992, p.192).

It is not always possible, or even desirable, however, for a bank to rely entirely on NGOs to do this work. Firstly, of course, in some areas there are no NGOs operating at all, and if On-Lending Groups really are an avenue to a large, new and potentially profitable market bankers should not adopt a purely passive attitude, waiting for an NGO to bring them readymade customers.

Secondly, even if there are NGOs which are working in community development, they may not be willing or able to promote groups effectively. Many NGOs are poorly managed, and are particularly weak at record-keeping and financial management and some, even today, still regard bankers as the natural enemies of the poor. This may not matter if they are working in areas such as community empowerment, health or education, particularly if they are funded by individual well-wishers, or even by their workers themselves, who are confident that their time and money will be well spent. Work with On-Lending Groups, however, requires business skills and business-like attitudes. The groups must keep simple but accurate records, and must manage their finances properly. An NGO which cannot do these things for itself is unlikely to be able to assist others to do them.

The low cost of NGO staff may also be reflected in the low quality of their work. Some Village Bank promotion agencies (Holt, 1994, p.174) have found that community workers are not always less expensive than financial professionals, because they lack financial training, and they also lack the "clout" which is necessary to pressure groups and promote discipline.

We have already shown that there are large numbers of informal groups in most communities, which have experience in regular saving, and in some form of lending. Bankers who operate in areas where there are no suitable NGOs should market their savings facilities aggressively to existing groups, and should then seek out potential borrowers from those groups whose savings record demonstrates that they have the need and the ability to make use of bank finance. One of the most difficult parts of this marketing task may be to overcome the group members' negative perception of banks. Once this has been achieved, it should be possible to mobilise significant new deposits and to develop profitable new customers for advances.

NGO Group Development and Assessment—Parivartan, Kalahandi

Parivartan is an NGO which operates in Kalahandi, the poorest district of Orissa, and thus one of the poorest places in the whole of India. The NGO has promoted a total of 67 groups in less than three years. At first, group development was undertaken by four field staff, in addition to their other work in education, health and community development. Latterly, 14 of the NGO's 31 field staff have been engaged in group development and support, but they also have responsibility for the other activities. Parivartan staff have to work with new groups intensively for between four and six months before they are able to save regularly. Thereafter, it is still necessary to make brief visits to the groups twice a month.

Oxfam, an international NGO, has provided two grants of Rs 10000 and Rs 15000 to support the group development work, but it is impossible to make any accurate estimate of the cost of this specific activity of Parivartan, since it is so closely integrated with all their other activities.

The local banks were at first very reluctant even to open savings accounts for the groups, and this problem has by no means been overcome. As a result of Parivartan's work, however, a total of five groups have now been able to borrow a total of Rs. 110000, or about US$3150, from the Kalahandi Rural Bank. The bank has required Parivartan to guarantee the loans, and has never visited the groups. The whole effort and expense of group development and assessment has been undertaken by the NGO, at virtually no expense to the bank.

Conclusion

As with so many questions, the answer to this must be "it depends". If there is a competent NGO, with a successful track record in developing and assessing groups, which is willing to collaborate with a bank, it would obviously be uneconomic for the bank to try to duplicate this expertise.

Many NGOs are neither willing nor able to work in this field, however, and because microfinance is so fashionable, there is also a danger that NGOs will try to become involved in the promotion of On-Lending Groups when they have neither the skills nor the attitudes which are necessary.

Banks must therefore be selective; it is notoriously difficult to appraise NGOs, because of their multiple goals and their heavy dependence on particular people. Basix Finance, whose experimental group rating system has already been mentioned, is also developing an assessment system for collaborating NGOs. The organisation's human resources and experience in financial services are given the most weight, but in the final analysis such decisions must depend on managerial judgement and not on quantitative ratings.

If there are no suitable NGOs serving the area covered by a particular branch, this does not mean that the branch cannot enter this new market. This study has identified numerous examples of banks which have successfully developed On-Lending Groups; this has usually been at the initiative of an individual branch manager, often in spite of lack of interest or even obstruction from his superiors. Some of these examples have depended on uniquely committed and devoted managers, but it is possible for bank branches to develop successful groups without such unusual people. What is needed is commitment and enthusiasm from senior management. This should be primarily motivated not by concern for social responsibility or public relations, but by a sincere belief that these groups represent a profitable business opportunity.

4.4. What Interest Rate can On-Lending Groups Afford to Pay ?

The banks in India charge 12% annual interest on their loans to On-Lending Groups, and K-Rep charges 35%; these rates were not fixed by the market, or by any reference to what the groups were willing and able to pay, nor were they based on any assessment of the transaction or financial costs of the respective lenders.

The K-Rep rate of 35% was already earlier being charged to group enterprises, which had a poor repayment record, and to solidarity groups of the Grameen Bank, Bangladesh type, which involve very high transaction costs because the lender deals individually with each loan and the group acts only as a guarantor and facilitator, not as a micro-banking intermediary. The group on-lending was started at the request of some women who ran a group enterprise, but asked if they could use their group loan for their individual businesses. The K-Rep field officer accepted their request as an experiment, and they naturally paid the same rate of interest as they had for their group enterprise loan.

The Indian rate of 12% is part of what little remains of the totally regulated interest rate regime which used to be imposed on all the banks by the Reserve Bank of India. Commercial banks are still not allowed to set their own interest rates on loans for under Rs. 20,000, or about $570, although the cooperative and the regional rural banks are now free to charge whatever interest rate they wish even on the smallest loans. Loans to On-Lending Groups are, however, refinanced by NABARD at the heavily subsidised rate of 6.5%, but this refinance is only available if it is on-lent at no more than 12%. This low cost refinance allows the banks to make a reasonable spread even if they on-lend at 12%, so this has become the normal rate for group lending.

The new Indian microfinance NGOs which are borrowing from SIDBI are however lending to On-Lending Groups at 15% interest, rather than the 12% charged by the banks, but the groups have had no difficulty in paying this higher rate. Basix Finance, in Andhra Pradesh, is charging groups 18% interest, even though there are branches of regional rural banks and commercial banks which are convenient to the groups' locations, and which could, were they so inclined, lend to the same groups at 12%. These banks do not market their services to such customers, however, and are not perceived as having any inclination to deal with them. It is now widely accepted that access to credit is more important for small borrowers than its cost; On-Lending Groups' priorities appear to be no different.

K-Rep originally envisaged that On-Lending Groups would add a margin to the 35% which they had to pay for their loans when they on-lend to their members, and some groups did indeed do this; there was high inflation at that time in Kenya, and interest rates were generally much higher than in 1997, when the study was undertaken. All the On-Lending Groups which were covered in this study are now merely passing on the 35% rate to their members, without adding any margin. They do make other charges to cover their administrative costs, but they claim that their members would not be able to repay if the interest charges were any higher.

The Kenyan On-Lending Group members are generally dealing with larger sums than their Indian counterparts, so they might be expected to be less able to pay high interest rates, but It still appears that there is a fairly wide band of uncertainty; Groups can pay 12%, or even 15% or 18%, without difficulty, but 35% is around the limit. If banks are to enter this market on the basis of its potential for profits, rather than in response to subsidy or exhortation, they need to have some idea of the price that the market will bear.

The price groups can pay of course depends on what they can charge. The On-Lending Groups which were studied in India charged between 60% and 18% annual interest to their members. The 19 groups where it was possible to ascertain the on-lending rate, charged as follows:

1 Group charged 18%
9 Groups charged 24%
5 Groups charged 30%
1 Group charged 36%
1 Group charged 50%
2 Groups charged 60%

Four other On-Lending Groups charged variable rates, depending on the use to which the money was to be put; the others charged the same rate regardless of purpose.

Only four of these nineteen groups chose to charge more than the 35% charged by K-Rep in Kenya, which implies that the limit of acceptability may not be so different in the two countries. Almost half of them, however, were charging 30% or more; this suggests that Indian banks could charge more than the present 12% without meeting any resistance. The experience of the SIDBI funded NGOs, and of Basix Finance, confirms that some increase is possible, if it is necessary to cover the initial investment required for appraisal, or even for the whole process of development if there are no NGOs willing and able to provide this service free of charge.

The ability of On-Lending Groups to pay a given rate for funds depends on their members' ability in turn to pay at least the same rate for their loans from the group, as in the case of K-Rep's groups, or a higher rate as is adopted by all the Indian groups. This ability depends on the rate they can earn from the investments they make with the money.

Our study did not extend to the economics of the group members' businesses, except in one or two isolated cases, but extensive data are available on the rate of return that is earned on the total capital invested in micro-enterprise, for about over 200 micro-enterprises in India and Kenya. This has been collected during student field work assignments. The businesses were of all types, and they were selected at random by the students along roadsides, in villages and in urban markets. About one-third of the businesses, which tended to be the smaller ones, were owned by women.

The sample is not representative of all micro-enterprises, and some On-Lending Group members, particularly in Kenya, are running more substantial businesses where the rates of return are lower. The figures are, however, typical of the smallest micro-enterprises everywhere, and their owners are those whose ability to pay should be of concern. All the earnings figures were adjusted for seasonality, and an estimate was made of what the owner would have earned had she or he not owned the business, in order to give an approximation of the incremental earnings which resulted from the fact that the owner had invested some capital in her or his own business, rather than having to be employed by somebody else. For rural people the alternative work, or opportunity cost of labour, was usually casual farm labour, possibly some distance from home, and for city dwellers it was portering, domestic service, garbage picking or other casual work.

The following figures summarise the results of analysis of these data for 215 micro-enterprises:

Average annual net incremental return on investment	847%
Range of rates of net return	Minus 480% to plus 19200%
Number of cases with net return under 100%	40 cases
Number of cases with net return over 1000%	44 cases
Number of cases with negative net return	10 cases

These figures are at first sight surprising. Even large businesses are judged to be very profitable if the annual return on the capital invested in them exceeds 30%

and successful investors in the stock market make around 25% on their portfolios. Every reader who has weven a passing acquaintance with a vegetable vendor, a village artisan or a roadside hawker, however, will realise that these figures are typical. The investments are so small that even earnings which are well below the poverty line represent a very high rate of return on them.

These returns do not of course mean that the owners of these enterprises are richer than stock market investors. Their investments are very small, so that the actual earnings are still very low and the owners are often still very poor, even if they are earning what appear to be astronomic returns on their investments. The figures do mean, however, that people who wish to start micro-enterprises can afford to pay very high rates of interest for the small sums of capital they need. The difference between 12% and 35% annual interest is of little significance to someone who can earn 100% or even 1000% on her investment; what matters is to be able to obtain the funds as and when the opportunity and the need arises.

Applicants for membership of the Kenyan On-Lending Groups are usually required already to have a business. Although there is no evidence of such a re-quirement in any of the Indian groups, many if not most of their members are engaged in petty trade when they join. It may therefore be fairer to examine the incremental rates of return not on the total capital invested in a micro-enterprise, but on expansion capital that the owner invests to improve her earnings.

Table 21 gives the data for four typical cases in India; an egg vendor who freed herself from dependence on a moneylender for her daily working capital, a tailor who added a small range of ready-made garments to her usual custom business, a puffed rice maker who was able to buy twice as much paddy to process as before, and a pedal rickshaw driver who bought his own rickshaw and thus saved the six-dollar daily rental fee.

These incremental rates of return on expansion investments are significantly lower than those achieved over the whole enterprise, but they are probably more

Table 21. Rates of Return on Expansion Investments

Business	Present monthly earnings	Extra capital needed	Projected earnings	Addition to earnings	Annual return on investment
Egg vending	$ 50	$ 20 to avoid the moneylender	$ 75	$ 25	600%
Rickshaw	$ 30	$ 200 to buy rickshaw	$ 36	$ 6	240%
Puffed rice making	$ 10	$ 40 to buy raw material	$ 20	$ 10	1200%
Tailor	$ 60	$ 50 for cloth for readymades	$ 80	$ 20	396%

typical of the types of investment made by On-Lending Group members. Even if a significant allowance is made for the costs of failure, the rates of return are still well in excess of any interest charge that is likely to be levied by a group on its members.

On-Lending Group members also borrow for so-called "consumption" purposes, where no financial return can be directly ascribed to the investment. Many groups start by making such loans, because they are smaller in amount and more urgent that loans for productive enterprise. If banks restrict the use of their money to 'productive' purposes, On-Lending Groups may continue to use their own savings for consumption lending. Such loans are in many cases the most urgently required, and are also, for that reason, the most expensive to obtain from a moneylender.

For most On-Lending Group members, the moneylender is the alternative to borrowing from their group. Although moneylenders' interest rates are often exaggerated, even secured loans rarely cost less than three per cent a month, and the rates for very small urgent loans, for very poor people, may be as much as ten per cent a day. Given the cost of the alternative, therefore, we can conclude that group members can afford to pay similarly high rates for consumption loans as for loans which are to be invested in their businesses.

Interest and Rates of Return—Musangi's hair salon

Felistus Musangi started his hair salon business in 1993. He is a member of the Tumaini group in Machakos, and has taken two loans from the group, to pay for new equipment to improve and expand his business.
On 29.2.97 his balance sheet was approximately as follows:

Balance sheet, or statement of financial condition

Assets		Liabilities	
Furniture and eqpt.	Ksh. 100300	Capital	Ksh. 100000
Material stocks	Ksh. 24000	K-Rep Loan	Ksh. 48000
Debtors	Ksh. 9000	Accumulated surplus	Ksh. 58300
Bank balance	Ksh. 64000		
Cash	Ksh. 9000		
Total	Ksh. 206300	Total	Ksh. 206300

His operating statement for the month of February 1997 was approximately as follows:

Sales Revenue	Ksh. 60000
Wages, hair care products and other expenses	Ksh. 13300
Profit including Musangi's salary	Ksh. 46700

Musangi paid his one employee about Ksh. 8000 a month, and he drew about Ksh. 20,000 for his own salary. This was about twice what he could have earned if he had been employed in another salon instead of running his own business. The monthly return on the total investment of Ksh 206,300 in his business was thus Ksh. 46,700 minus Ksh. 10,000 (the "opportunity cost" of his labour), or Ksh. 36,700. This was equivalent to nearly 18% a month, or 215% a year. This was over six times the annual interest rate of 35% which he paid to the Tumaini group, and which the group in turn paid to K-Rep. The profitability of Musangi's business was about average for the members of his group.

Conclusion

We can therefore conclude with some confidence that members can afford to pay what appear to be very high rates of interest for loans from their On-Lending Groups. As their businesses expand, they will become more capital-intensive and the rates of return will drop as the absolute amounts increase. At this point, they may be able to borrow individually, from an existing commercial bank or from the new microfinance institution which served their group and has moved up to serve the emerging needs of its "graduates" as well as its groups. At the micro-level, however, there is more than adequate economic 'space' for the group and any bank which has the vision to lend to it.

4.5. How can On-Lending Groups Provide Security ?

One of the main reasons why banks are reluctant to deal with poorer people, unless it be to take their savings deposits at a low rate of interest, and to lend them on to richer people at a higher one, is that the poor are indeed poor. Poverty means lack of assets, and bankers prefer to lend money to people who already have it, in some form which can be pledged as security in case of default. The lender may reduce his transaction costs by lending to groups rather than individuals, but a group of poor people do not acquire security by the act of being in a group.

Group intermediation does, of course, mobilise social pressure. This can take the form of mutual assistance and support in case of hardship, or it may be as ruthless as any bailiff, as the examples which we referred to from Bangladesh show all too clearly. If pressure is unavailing, however, a group guarantee is worth no more than the aggregated assets of the group. If they are all poor, and if several suffer loss at the same time, their joint assets will not be likely to cover their debts. The type of assets which poor people own are also likely to be portable, or easily sold at short notice. If a group decide to default *en masse*, they will easily be able to make their few possessions inaccessible to a formal financial institution.

Although some banks do make unsecured loans, this is exceptional and is usually done only for clients who have an established track record and are known to have sufficient wealth to cover their obligations. Much of the security taken by banks is in practice unrealisable, but the threat of seizure is a powerful incentive for repayment, and auditors' formal appraisals of the value of a loan portfolio often take little account of the feasibility of seizure or disposal of securities. If banks are to regard On-Lending Groups as serious customers, the issue of security must be dealt with.

It can be argued that poor people need convenient, flexible and secure savings facilities as much as they need credit, and that the poorest people need such facilities more than they need loans (Rutherford, 1995). If this is true, their aggregate savings will exceed their borrowing requirement, and the group mechanism can ensure that the amount outstanding in loans will be covered by their total savings. The need for flexibility and easy access to savings, however, mean that any fund which attempted to use members' deposits as 100% security for their loans would have problems of matching maturities. Only a large institution which could intermediate between the needs of people over a wide area and avoid co-variant risks would be able to overcome the practical difficulties of ensuring that outstanding loans were at all times matched by deposits.

Although commercial banks have traditionally taken deposits from poorer savers to be lent to richer borrowers, the market for savings instruments continues to be neglected. Many rural banks in India still refuse to take deposits from groups, even though the Reserve Bank specifically authorised them to do so in January 1993 (PRADAN, 1996). In Indonesia in 1984, a change in the law made it possible for groups to open accounts in their group names rather than in the leader's own name. This "opened a large new market for rural deposits" (Robinson, 1994, p.37), and the banks responded enthusiastically.

The AKRSP in northern Pakistan makes loans to the Village Organisations and Women's Organisations only up to the level of their own savings deposits in the bank. Within the groups too, each member is only allowed to take a loan up to the amount of her own savings, unless she can persuade another member who does not need to borrow up to her own limit to guarantee the balance. This rule is not always observed in practice, but the total amount extended to a group cannot exceed its total savings. The AKRSP system is however unusual, and totally uncommercial, in that the groups earn 12% interest on their savings deposits with the local commercial bank. but they only pay 7% interest to AKRSP (Harper A, 1995 p.47). They therefore make a 5% surplus just by taking a loan, regardless of whether and how the funds are lent out.

Institutions with a greater concern for their own sustainability have adopted a variety of strategies to deal with the issue of security, but they necessarily involve compromising the principle of 100% coverage. The proportions of savings which are demanded as security by a selection of microfinance institutions when they are lending to On-Lending Groups or similar intermediaries, are as follows:

Most Credit Unions (Magill J, 1994, p.47)	33% to 50%
SANASA Sri Lanka (SANASA, 1994)	33%
PHBK, Indonesia (32)	25%
Cashbank South Africa (Cashbank, 1993)	25%
BRI Indonesia (Foundation for Development Cooperation, 1992, p.38)	25% (for credit unions)
Rastriya Banija Bank, Nepal (Ogunleye, 1996)	5%
K-Rep, Kenya	10%

This is a wide range, and each institution also uses the security in a different way. At one extreme, the required proportion of savings may merely be required as an equivalent of the micro-bank's owners' equity. The lender will not demand or expect that the funds should be kept on deposit, or even shown to exist as cash. The On-Lending Group has only to show from its records that it has the required value of assets, most or all of which are already lent out to its members.

Alternatively, the lender may require the funds to be shown in cash, to demonstrate that the loans are recoverable, but may then allow the money to be lent out again along with its own loan. More usually, the security has to be deposited with the bank, but here again the terms will differ. If the required proportion of the loan has to be kept in a low interest demand deposit, but mandated to the bank, this effectively increases the rate of interest paid by the group, as well as preventing them from using their own money. If the security can be kept in a time deposit, which earns a higher rate of interest, this is less onerous, but the rate of return will inevitably be far below what the members themselves could earn by investing the funds in micro-enterprise.

NABARD suggest that banks should start by limiting loans to On-Lending Groups to twice their savings, or even to the same amount as their savings, and suggests that the multiple should be increased after favourable experience to four or more times. The decision as to whether the savings amount should merely be seen to exist, or whether it should be kept on deposit as security, is left to the banks.

Most banks in Orissa insist on the savings being kept on deposit, and this of course seriously limits the funds at the group's disposal. If the bank has insisted on a 1:1 ratio, and if the whole sum of the group's savings must remain on deposit until the complete loan is cleared, the group will of course have less money to lend out to its members, throughout the repayment period of the bank loan.

It is more usual for On-Lending Groups to be required to deposit half the amount they are borrowing on their first loan. One group borrowed Rs. 20,000, which was repaid over twelve months at 12% interest. They had to deposit Rs. 10,000, at 9% interest, and this was blocked for the full twelve months. During half the nominal period of the loan, the bank was actually indebted to the group. Nevertheless, this apparently illogical situation is accepted, because it is viewed as a qualifying period for more reasonable terms. Although the bank had nominally only taken 50% security, it was of course well covered for half the period. NABARD also suggests short maturities, and many groups repay their early smaller loans within a few weeks or months, so that the hardship is less than it might appear.

K-Rep requires every On-Lending Group to deposit 10% of its loan in a demand deposit at a commercial bank, which is mandated to K-Rep and cannot be withdrawn until the loan is completely cleared. A K-Rep Credit Officer or area manager is appointed as a signatory to the account. These deposits are not usually withdrawn by the groups, since the usual practice is to proceed from one loan to another, usually for a larger amount. K-Rep does not hesitate to use its authority to cover late payments from the groups' deposits. When this happens, members are made forcibly aware of their groups' arrears, and of the members which have caused them. This has lead to the break-up of some groups, but K-Rep's losses have been minimised.

Groups themselves can impose sanctions against defaulting members which are more onerous and immediate than a bank could use. It is most unlikely that a group would fail to repay the bank if all its members had repaid the group, so banks should consider the security arrangements between the groups and their members as well as between themselves and the groups. They may not be legally enforceable, but they are at the same time often far more powerful in practice than anything a bank could do.

Within the On-Lending Groups themselves, individual borrowers pledge marketable assets such as radios or television sets, sewing machines, bicycles or cooking vessels to their groups as security for repayment, and in Kenya these pledges are often legally certified by law through a sworn affidavit which is executed by a commissioner for oaths. These arrangements are made at the discretion and expense of the groups themselves, but they clearly have a positive if indirect influence on their loan repayments to K-Rep. Other groups may not specify particular assets as security, but they are not slow to seize defaulters' possessions when they believe that a borrower's failure to pay is wilful rather than the result of circumstances beyond her control.

On-Lending Groups can and do exert more effective pressure for recovery than banks, but they are also able to help their members in more positive ways. One member of the BR Ambedkar group in Uttar Pradesh borrowed Rs. 1500 to buy a sewing machine, but it was stolen. Her fellow-members knew that she was a reliable person and could develop a good market for her tailoring. They agreed to lend her a further Rs. 1500, so that she could replace the stolen machine, and she was able to repay both loans from the additional income she made with the machine. Very few banks would have had the necessary local knowledge to make a similar decision.

Security and repayment—The Mahila Sanchaya Samiti

The Sanchaya Samiti women's group started with the help of an NGO called Samuha Vikash in Kerasingh village, a tribal community in Orissa, early in 1994. There are 16 members; the secretary has been to school and can keep simple records, but the other members can do no more than count their own savings.

Each member saves Rs. 5 every month. Sometimes one or two fail to bring their savings by the agreed deadline of the 19th of the month, but when they are late they have to pay a one rupee fine. They also made a special collection of Rs. 50 each, or a total of Rs. 800, to augment their funds.

For the first five months , the members only saved; they wanted to accumulate a reasonable fund before they started to take loans. They deposited their savings in the Bahadajhola branch of the Bank of Baroda. By the end of 1996 they had saved Rs. 3420, plus Rs. 40 from fines. They also earned about Rs. 2000 through group forest-based activities such as collecting tamarind and leaves for making disposable plates.

They had started borrowing from the fund after the initial five month period, and they charged themselves 2% a month on their loans. In August 1996 they took a loan from the Bank of Baroda for Rs. 3500; they deposited the same amount from their own funds in the bank.

By February 1997 the total capital of the group amounted to almost Rs. 10,000 from their own savings, the bank loan, the interest earned on their loans and the bank interest. Their loan repayments were up-to-date, and the bank was ready to advance a second loan of double their own savings, because of the complete success of the first loan.

Conclusion

The on-time repayment record of On-Lending Groups is better than most banks are used to even with corporate customers. The experience with advances to public sector institutions, to small businesses and farmers and particularly with loans to poorer people under government sponsored schemes has been far worse. It may therefore seem unnecessary to discuss the issue of security, since most banks make some unsecured loans, and these groups appear to merit similar treatment.

Nevertheless, bankers are rightly cautious, and there is a natural tendency to find one reason why a new thing should not be done than to find many reasons why it should. As the above example shows, some On-Lending Groups are willing and able to provide 100% security in the form of savings deposits, and even to allow the whole sum to remain on deposit until they have completely cleared their loan.

This is clearly not tenable in the long term, however; once a group has established a good track record it is reasonable for them to expect to be "graduated" and to borrow two, four or even ten times their savings. Continuing one hundred per cent security is not in practice attainable. The repayment rates which have been achieved by banks which have properly managed their lending to On-Lending Groups suggest that such coverage is not necessary, but bankers must recognise that this new customer group will have to be treated differently from their normal customers.

CHAPTER 5

THE FUTURE

5.1. What is Stopping the Banks ?

The record so far

We have already seen that in addition to the banks covered by our study, a few other commercial banks are already doing some business with On-Lending Groups. Habib Bank in Pakistan, Hatton National Bank in Sri Lanka and the Bank of the Philippine Islands are not major multinational institutions. They are, however, well-established national banks, not so unlike hundreds of similar institutions worldwide which have so far apparently not recognised this new market opportunity.

A number of newer private banks and non-bank finance institutions have already become involved, in Bangladesh, Indonesia (Dixit, 1996) and elsewhere (Rutherford and Arora, 1997), imitating the public or "development" sector institutions, but for profit. The microfinance industry in general is of course expanding rapidly, but the vast majority of the activity is fuelled by grants and subsidised funds. Only a small part of the industry is genuinely and wholly commercial, and whatever growth is taking place in that part is mainly being driven by new private institutions, rather than by the established commercial banks. In Indonesia, for instance, new small private banks are working with On-Lending Groups as way of developing new individual customers as well as profitable business in own right.

The On-Lending Group business examined in this study is not strictly commercial, in that the funds which are lent by banks in India are refinanced at a heavily subsidised rate by NABARD, and K-Rep's finance has thus far been provided mainly by donors, free of charge. Nevertheless, the Indian commercial banks are first and foremost commercial institutions which have to make a profit to survive. Most of them are nationalised, and have a strong social mandate, but in recent years in particular they have been compelled to put profits first. Their behaviour in relation to the On-Lending Group market, or any other new field, can therefore be examined as a case of commercial decision-making, which is not too heavily distorted by non-business motives. Their on-lending rate to groups has also been limited as a condition of their access to NABARD refinance, but the total spread is probably not very different from what they might expect if they were using "real" money, and lending it on to groups for whatever they were willing to pay.

The Kenyan situation is quite different, in that the commercial banks are more or less totally uninvolved, but a number of NGOs have entered the market in a fairly significant way. Most of their funds are like K-Rep's, free or heavily subsidised, but they have been able to lend to On-Lending Groups at very high rates of interest, and thus accumulate a substantial surplus as the beginnings of an equity base for financial independence. Their projections suggest that this business will continue to be profitable, even as an increasing proportion of their funds has to be raised on the commercial market. Nevertheless, the Kenyan commercial banks, whether foreign or locally owned, have shown no interest in this apparently profitable field.

The level of market penetration the NGOs have achieved in Kenya, although very small, is actually almost four times that which has been achieved in India by all the banks and NGOs put together (Table 22).

Table 22: Market Penetration, India and Kenya

	India	Kenya
Approx. population	1 billion	25 million
Approx. no. of groups linked	20,000	1850
Members reached (@ 20 per group)	400,000	37,000
Per cent of population	0.04%	0.148%

The figures for India in Table 22 include the On-Lending Groups which have been financed by NGOs which have themselves borrowed from SIDBI or other sources, as well as those which have been linked directly with the banks; the figures would be even less impressive if they only included the "pure" cases, where a group has borrowed directly from a bank.

If we regard women as the main target market, the comparison would be even less favourable to India, because in India the proportion of women in the total population, at 48%, is lower than in Kenya (50.4%), or in nearly every other country for that matter. The reasons for this deplorable situation are beyond the scope of discussion here, but improved access to financial services is one of the ways in which it may eventually be remedied.

The rate of growth in India has accelerated, but not dramatically. The following figures give the numbers of On-Lending Groups which borrowed money from commercial banks in each of the four years from 1992, when NABARD first announced its programme to promote this form of intermediation:

Year	Number of groups borrowing
1992-93	255
1993-94	365
1994-95	1502
1995-96	2635
1996-97	about 3750
Total	about 8507

Most loans to On-Lending Groups are for three years, so only a small number of these groups may be double-counted because they have borrowed more than once during this six-year period.

Twenty-eight commercial banks, sixty Regional Rural Banks and seven co-operative banks were involved in these transactions, and many branches financed several groups. There are, however, about 75,000 commercial and rural bank branches in India, quite apart from the even larger network of district and primary level cooperative bank outlets. Even if each of these 8,500 On-Lending Groups was the only one which had been financed by its respective branch, this would mean that barely 11% of the nation's bank branches have so much as dipped their toes into this new market place. In fact, of course, a far smaller number of branches have actually been involved. The 778 groups in Orissa which had borrowed from banks up to 31.3.97, for instance, were financed by a total of 42 branches, from 18 banks. This is less than 2% of the bank branches in the State.

MYRADA estimated (Foundation for Development Cooperation, 1992) that about 15 million On-Lending Groups would be needed to reach all the poor in India. It can be argued that this figure is too large, but even if it is ten times too optimistic, the rate of growth has been lamentable. If a commercial supplier of any product or service estimated that there was a national market of this scale, and after five years his sales had reached so small a number, either his market research staff or his sales staff would be fired. What has gone wrong?

Some Reasons why banks should work with On-Lending Groups

The Foundation for Development Cooperation, in the report which has already been cited, stated that, "...there is no reason why the banking community of Asia, including the commercial banks, should not be able to meet a substantial portion of the loan capital requirement" (ibid., p.31).

The Reserve Bank of India issued a further circular on Self-Help Group financing in April 1996, in order to deal with some issues that had arisen in the four years' previous experience. It suggested that the banks should treat the group linkage programme "as a business opportunity", a "normal lending activity" and "part of their mainstream credit operations".

The commercial banks in India still look to the Central Bank for guidance on issues which in many countries would be dealt with by each bank, or even by each branch, so the circular specifically stated that banks need not be constrained if the husbands of some group members had defaulted on previous loans. This is a relevant issue in India, because of the massive defaults that have been experienced on ill-designed and mismanaged poverty alleviation schemes. The circular also specified that the banks might if they wished extend overdrafts or "cash credit limits" to groups, rather than term loans; the subsidised refinance would still be made available. The banks could hardly claim that there were any remaining regulatory barriers to prevent or even discourage them from doing business with On-Lending Groups (PRADAN, 1996, pp. 23-25).

The major initial benefit to a bank which seeks out On-Lending Groups as customers will probably be from deposit mobilisation. The average savings of the groups in the four Indian states was Rs. 17,000, or about $480, and the figure for the Kenyan groups was Ksh. 93,500, or about $1700. These are large sums in the context of rural branches, in India and Kenya, and new business of this magnitude would presumably be welcome to any bank, anywhere.

The early loans are not large, since On-Lending Group members' absorption capacity has been limited both by lack of opportunities but also by their previous lack of access to reasonably priced finance. First loans to groups in India typically range between Rs. 2000 and Rs. 10,000, or $60 to $300, but the amounts can rise rapidly as both sides gain confidence and the members' horizons broaden. PRADAN believe that a typical "Kalanjian" group in Tamil Nadu can after three to four years make profitable use of a loan for as much as three hundred thousand rupees, or $8500. The members rapidly graduate from very small consumption credits to loans for petty trade, rice processing or one or two goats, and then to more substantial finance for dairy cows, poultry units or land lease (Pradan 1996 p.45).

The scale of the deposits and advances is attractive, but there are also other powerful reasons why bankers in India and Kenya, and in many other countries, should welcome this new business with enthusiasm. Taking a bank loan has come to be perceived in some places not as a mutually profitable business transaction between the bank and the its customer, but as a form of patronage or reward for political or similar services. If loans are given to a group rather than an individual, and particularly to a group of poor people, the political implications of lending to individuals are reduced (NABARD-APRACA, 1996, p.90).

The recovery experience on group loans has not been perfect, but it has been very much better than the experience on personal, small business and corporate enterprise. In Orissa (Panda and Mishra, 1996, p.36) the banks have recovered 88% of all instalments from On-Lending Groups loans on the due date or before, and the remaining arrears have generally been settled shortly thereafter. The same branches had an overall recovery rate of 77%, and the rate was as low as 36% on loans to the communities where they are now doing business with On-Lending Groups. K-Rep's experience in Kenya has been similar. Their auditors have agreed that a figure of 2.5% is sufficient for bad debt provision, and although there have been some cases of group default, as already described, the overall experience has been positive.

The costs and the returns

A banker, like any businessman, should only take on a new customer if the relationship will be a profitable one. The initial investment in marketing, promotion and assessment must eventually be covered by the profits which will be earned. We saw earlier that it cost a bank in India about $20 to assess a group which had been promoted by a NGO, and that the cost of the promotion function was about $200. The Kenyan groups have generally been initiated and developed by their own members, so that the remaining promotion task is substantially less than in India; the cost of this, and of assessment, is again around $200.

Twenty dollars is a small investment to make in order to acquire a customer of the scale and potential of an On-Lending Group, irrespective of the fact that a number of individual customers may in due course "graduate" from the group. It seems clear, therefore, that any banker who is interested in profitable business should welcome On-Lending Groups if they present themselves, or are presented by NGOs, as "ready-made", clients which only have to be assessed. The evidence from India suggests that most bankers are in fact unwilling to recognise this.

The case is less clear if the bank is required to invest not only the cost of assessment but also that of promotion and development. Two hundred dollars may seem to be a high price to pay to acquire one customer, but an average group has about 20 members. Ten dollars seems a reasonable acquisition cost for one customer, even a very small one, given the high recovery rates and the potential for growth. The case would be much clearer, however, if the potential business with the group was more profitable, in terms of interest rates, than other more familiar transactions.

We have already seen that On-Lending Groups can easily afford to pay rates of interest that are not only higher than the subsidised rate of 12% which is normal in India, but are also higher than the Indian "market" rate of approximately 18%. One major reason why banks in India, and in Kenya and elsewhere, are unwilling to enter this market, and indeed the microfinance market in general, is that they are reluctant to charge interest rates which may appear usurious, especially to poorer people. The borrowers themselves will not complain, since their alternative source of finance, if they have one at all, is moneylenders, and the "market" rate was never available to them. Government, politicians, shareholders and the public at large may well object, however, and the risk of damage to the banks' image may outweigh the potential profits.

The Regional Rural Banks in India are now allowed to charge whatever rate of interest they choose on even the smallest loans, and the same freedom may be expected soon to be given to the national commercial banks, as the last vestiges of interest rate regulation disappear. The Cooperative Banks have also had the same freedom, for a rather longer period, but they have generally not been involved in financing On-Lending Groups. People who have been imprisoned for long periods are often frightened of freedom, however, and the same may apply to bankers, at the branch or at higher levels, who have never been free to make decisions on interest rates.

The banks in India are able to lend to On-Lending Groups at 12% because they can refinance the loans at 6.5%. This 5.5% "spread", however, is for some banks much less than the difference between their average cost of funds, which was said in 1997 to be as low as 8.2% for India's largest bank, and the "market" rate of 18%. The profits would be greater if they were willing to lend to groups at the higher rates which are quite normal for microfinance institutions.

There were, however, no cases where Regional Rural Banks were making use of their new freedom and lending to groups from their own funds, rather than using refinance, and there seems little possibility that the national banks will be any more aggressive when they are free to set their own interest rates. It may be that bankers will only enter this market on a large scale when the very existence of their institutions, and their own jobs, depend on their success in finding new and profitable opportunities for business. In India, this threat is not yet recognised.

One case was found where a cooperative bank was taking advantage of its freedom to lend at higher rates. The Sambalpur District Central Cooperative Bank, in northern Orissa, made two loans, for Rs. 10,000 and Rs. 30,000, to On-Lending Groups at 17% interest. The same bank had lent Rs. 3000 to another group at 12.5% the previous year; it was not clear whether the higher rate was charged because the bank could not obtain refinance or for some other reason. All three loans were repaid as per schedule, and there was no evidence that the groups, or the NGO which introduced the groups to the bank, objected to the higher rate.

K-Rep is not a bank, but its business with On-Lending Groups is substantial and the costs and revenues associated with it are quite easily separated from its other activities. This is probably the only example anywhere of a banking operation which is wholly devoted to this type of business, and its performance therefore provides valuable evidence as to how profitable it is.

The following figures show the approximate financial performance of this part of K-Rep for the calendar year 1996.

K-Rep's Credit Scheme: Consolidated income and expenditure Statement for the year ended 31 12 1996, in Kenyan shillings.

Income	
Service charge (interest)	71,805,184
Loan application fees	2,813,385
Registration fees	392,920
Passbook fees	308,565
Total	75,320,054
Interest on savings and deposit	6,383,869
Other income	929,855
Total Income	82,633,778
Expenditure	
Salaries	28,083,545
Office expenses	5,769,693
Depreciation	1,018,756
Training expenses	431,310
Travel and accommodation	2,773,872
Professional fees	751,740
Audit fees	600,000
Bad debt provision	7,988,950
Other expenses	3,904,239
Total expenses	51,322,105
Net Profit	31,311,673
@ Kshs 55 = US$ 1.00.....US$	569,303

The portfolio at the end of the year was Kshs. 269 million, or about five million dollars. This was not of course constant throughout the year, so that the above figures do not give an accurate picture of the average position throughout the period, but they do give an approximate indication of the operating economics. The actual loan loss experience is well under 2%, so the bad debt provision of around 3% is somewhat overstated.

One major omission, of course, is the cost of funds. K-Rep was not permitted to take deposits from its groups at this time, since it did not have a banking licence, and the majority of its funds consisted of grants for which no interest had to be paid. This profit of just over thirty million shillings approximates to about 11.6% on the total portfolio at the end of the year. If K-Rep had had to borrow these funds at the average interbank rate of about 18%, the cost would more than have absorbed the profit, and the operation would have run at a loss. If, however, K-Rep had been able to mobilise savings deposits from its clients like any other bank, they would have paid around 6% interest on these savings, plus around a further 4% for the administrative costs. The total of 10% would have been marginally less than the notional profit of 11.6% which was earned on the funds lent, so that the operation would have been in profit.

This example is of course hypothetical, because K-Rep is not a bank, and does not therefore enjoy many of the benefits, nor does it suffer from the costs, which are associated with commercial banking status. It does nevertheless suggest that banking through On-Lending Groups can be profitable in its own right.

Reasons why the banks should hesitate

We must recognise, however, that there may be some circumstances when banks should not enter this new market. In South Africa, for instance, it has been argued (Cashbank, 1993) that in the current situation of high mobility and exaggerated expectations banks would be wrong to enter this new and potentially volatile market. It would perhaps be wrong to put the banking system at risk, particularly since there are large numbers of NGOs and other organisations which are active in this area, and large sums of donor money to support them.

In Thailand the new village banks, which are similar to On-Lending Groups, are now borrowing from commercial banks with donor guarantees. NGOs such as CARE and FFH expect that their village banks will "graduate" to borrowing from the banks after six loan cycles, but doubts remain as to the advantages on either side. Holt (1994, p.177) questions the wisdom of such linkages in a country where the banking system is not performing well in other respects.

It can also be argued (Geertz, 1962, p.28) that ROSCAs and On-Lending Groups are only a temporary phenomenon, which bankers should attempt to replace rather than to serve. Houghton suggests (in Otero and Rhyne, 1994, p. vii) that it is part of the logic of microfinance that "private banks gravitate to large transactions with affluent borrowers and probably should not be expected to deliver small-size financial services to low-income clients." On-Lending Groups, and their members, may be so different from the markets to which banks are accustomed that they need new institutions to serve them; the newly recognised microfinance market may need new institutions to serve it.

Why are the banks not entering this Market ?

Whatever may be the arguments for new institutions, it seems clear that at least in some countries, and perhaps in most, the existing commercial banks ought to be addressing the On-Lending Group market more enthusiastically than they are. We must examine the constraints in order to identify which are susceptible to interventions such as training or organisation development, and which may be more soundly based and legitimate reasons for the banks' reluctance.

One problem may be that bankers are unaware of the existence of these groups. India particularly is a fiercely stratified society, and many bank managers and their staff have little or no personal experience or knowledge of the village or urban slum which may exist within a few meters of their home or office. They may claim (NABARD, 1995, p.30) that they suffer from "limitations of time and resources", but their "lack of enthusiasm to deal directly with a clientele characterised by poverty and illiteracy" may also inhibit them from serving this market. Local groups such as ROSCAs and chit funds with social and economic functions exist everywhere, in middle class and poorer communities, but managers who are well aware of their existence, and whose wives if not themselves are active members, often find it very difficult to perceive them as potential channels of distribution for financial services.

Group-based activities have also been discredited in India, Kenya and many other countries, because of the poor record of cooperative institutions. Many cooperatives have failed because too much was expected of them, or because people who are basically individualists are unwilling to submerge their own interests in a group. Official cooperatives have also tended to be dominated by men, whereas the On-Lending Group experience, and that of other group-based approaches to microfinance, suggests that women are better at working in groups than men. Whatever the reasons, however, the record is such that bankers are right to treat groups with some caution.

Our studies in India found that nearly all the branch managers who had financed groups had attended one of the many short training programmes which have been organised to introduce the banks to group lending and to inform them about refinance and other incentives. Many thousands of other Indian branch managers, and their seniors, have attended these programmes. Such exposure may be a necessary condition for expansion of the market, but it is not sufficient.

In most cases it is necessary for bankers to relate not only to one but to two new and unfamiliar business partners. On-Lending Groups themselves require new approaches to appraisal and management, but NGOs are also very different from the normal business or personal clients with which banks generally have to deal. A GEMINI report (1996, p.80) referred to the "...sometimes adversarial relationships between NGOs and government or more formal institutions...", which obviously includes banks. Many of the best NGOs are also local and small, and are jealous of their own approaches and management systems. Bankers who want standardised methods may be confused by this diversity.

Bankers may find it difficult to deal with NGOs, but they may be even more reluctant to undertake the minimal direct dealings with On-Lending Groups, even when they have been promoted, trained and even introduced by an NGO. They may therefore prefer to take the option of using the NGO as a further intermediary. In Kenya some commercial banks have taken this route, although at heavily subsidised rates of interest which suggest that the loans are more in the nature of public relations or social responsibility gestures than mainstream business.

Kenyan commercial banks and On-Lending Groups

The main commercial banks in Kenya have an extensive branch network in the rural and urban areas. One reason for their almost total failure to make any loans to On-Lending Groups may be that specialised micro-finance organisations such as K-Rep have preempted them. The banks may welcome this development because it absolves them from having to deal with what they may believe to be a fundamentally unprofitable market, or it may have prevented them from even considering the possibility from a commercial point of view, but the effect is the same.

Savings and Credit Groups, ROSCAs and merry-go-rounds are, however, an all-pervasive feature of Kenyan society, and there must be few women in particular who are not members of at least one such group. Many of these groups are of course good deposit customers of the banks, and have been for many years, but if such groups are also a natural intermediary for bank loans, and not just a means of mobilising savings, it is surprising that none of the banks has thus far considered the possibility of lending them money.

The only bank which was visited in our survey which is actively dealing with On-Lending Groups is the Kenya Cooperative Bank, which has so far given loans to eight groups in Meru district for a total of Kshs. 1.8 million, or about $33000. This is however a pilot experiment and is funded by DANIDA. The funds do not belong to the bank, which is only used as a delivery conduit. In spite of this, the groups still had to fulfil a number of conditions which are in some ways more stringent than those demanded by K-Rep. In addition to having official bye-laws and being account holders with the bank, their members must have had training in bookkeeping, credit administration, time management and group dynamics, and their savings must amount to 20% of the total amount of money to be borrowed, or twice the level demanded by K-Rep. The members must also agree to guarantee one another's debts.

The Kenya Family Bank, a smaller privately owned bank, also has a project funded by an international donor, whereby its Thika office makes loans to On-Lending Groups which have been developed and trained by the Kenya Enterprise Promotion Programme (KEPP). The funds do not belong to the bank, nor does the bank bear the risk of loss. The Bank does however appraise the loans, and does not necessarily accept KEPP's recommendations to lend.

The main business of this bank, however, is with coffee and tea farmers, rather than with urban small business people. KEPP is negotiating with another bank for which this type of business is closer to its main market, and it may be that this bank will be willing to take at least some share of the risk, since they do perceive the profit potential in doing business with these groups.

Barclays Bank and Kenya Commercial Bank both have special loans units which deal with micro- and small enterprises, but these units do not deal with On-Lending Groups.

The banks' representatives explained that their unwillingness to lend to On-Lending Groups was because such groups have certain weaknesses. They mentioned in particular the generally low levels of education of the members, which means that it takes them longer to understand and comply with the banks' lending procedures then other clients. This means that even when they are eligible to access credit, they cannot argue their cases clearly. The banks are also reluctant to lend to the groups because so many of their members are involved in agricultural activities which are by their nature risky.

The Nyahururu Cooperative Bank Manager also mentioned the difficulty of the groups' legal status. They are registered under the Societies Act rather than as companies, which means that their status and purposes are unclear and it is doubtful if they can be sued in case of default.

The bank staff argued that the transaction costs of loans to On-Lending Groups are too high, because they tend to be located at some distance from branches or headquarters, which involved the banks in time and costs for site visits. They also said that most groups were unable to keep proper accounts and audited statements with which their previous business performance could be analysed. They said that this financial information is essential for their lending decisions, and without it, they are unable to lend. They also said that the groups lacked collateral, and that their members found it difficult to agree on how their finances should be used. In general, the banks seemed to believe that most On-Lending Groups were badly managed, although it is quite clear from this study and others that many groups have excellent management and keep excellent up-to-date accounts.

The representatives of the Kenyan microfinance institutions had very different views as to the eligibility of On-Lending Groups for bank finance and they mentioned a number of specific cases. They believed that the high level of education of their members, and the types of business in which they were engaged meant that they were fully qualified for bank finance. CARE Kenya, however, were of the opinion that their would only be bankable if they received continuous follow-up.

Just over half of K-Rep's credit officers believed that groups which had been satisfactory K-Rep clients could successfully apply for bank loans. They mentioned factors such as the track record of prompt repayments which some groups had built up with K-Rep, their strong leadership, good management and the substantial capital and asset base which some groups have built up. Some groups have also been good savings customers of commercial banks for many years. All of these, they felt, were good reasons why banks should welcome them as customers. They felt, however, that about half of K-Rep's On-Lending Groups were not ready for bank loans. Some were too young to have built a track record, others were badly managed and had weak leadership, or their record of savings and repayments was poor.

Representatives of On-Lending Groups which worked with K-Rep were also asked whether they felt that their groups should be able to access bank loans. Some felt that their groups were ready to borrow from a bank, while the representatives of other groups said that they still had a long way to go. All were agreed, however, that even if they could, their groups have no intention of getting loans from the banks. Some said that they have as individuals tried to get bank loans, and will do so again in the future, but they felt that groups were not yet ready.

Group members' individual experiences and views

The above findings suggest that the banks have very negative views about groups as such. If On-Lending Groups are seen as a short-term "bridge" by which poorer people can reach the level of eligibility for formal finance, it may be that the banks are right to leave their financing to the other new institutions and to focus on those who "graduate" from the groups to become individual customers.

We therefore interviewed some group members in order to find out what stops them from trying to get credit from the banks. Their responses showed that some members have never even thought of approaching a bank, and others are quite ignorant about the banks' lending terms. Most of them, however, feel that they lack the necessary security. They generally have very negative views about the banks' lending conditions, which they feel are so harsh as completely to exclude people like themselves. Most of them relied on hearsay, however, and had not thought it was worthwhile to find out about the banks' conditions for themselves.

The following are brief extracts from members' responses to the question "why have you never approached a bank for a loan ?"

- The banks demand security for one to get a loan, I do not have any
- I hear the bank interest is high
- My business has not matured to a level where I can borrow from the bank
- I have never thought about it
- My business is not on a permanent business site. The municipal council can at any time chase me away. That restricts me from approaching a bank
- I have not seen the need
- My business does not require a lot of money
- I have never thought about approaching a bank
- I do not know the procedure of getting a loan from the bank
- I found out that the interest rate was too high for me
- If you do not repay a bank loan immediately, the bank auctions your things immediately
- I do not have any security for the loan
- I feared approaching them because I was not sure my business would progress well
- I did not see any need
- I do not have the means to access credit from the banks
- I did not have assets to act as security
- I fear to borrow from the bank

- I have no immediate use for a loan
- I lack security
- I am unable to meet their lending conditions
- I have never been interested in getting a loan from the banks
- I did not have a title deed for my land nor any other security
- The interest rate of the bank is too high
- I do not know the procedures of borrowing money from the bank
- I hear that the commercial banks normally require security yet I do not have any
- I do not have the security required by the banks
- I found the conditions too demanding
- I do not have a title deed for security
- Banks do not accept a group security
- I do not know the process involved in getting a loan from the bank
- I never thought about it
- I was already servicing another loan from a microfinance institution
- I did not even have a business
- Their interest rate is high
- Their rules are very tough so I have never attempted to get a loan
- I do not have any security at all
- I do not know how to approach them
- I have never thought about going to the bank
- I had security that was less what I wanted
- I do not have security such as a title deed
- I do not have an account with any of the banks
- I fear servicing two loans
- I think I have not yet qualified for a bank loan
- My level of business does not require a loan from the bank
- Their interest rate is high, secondly they ask for security which I do not have
- Lack of security to guarantee for the anticipated loan
- I never thought about it and in any case I do not have the security which they are going to ask me

These comments show why most group members have never approached a commercial bank for credit. It should be remembered that the respondents are business people, who are the future clients of commercial banks. Their feelings demonstrate the general failure of banks to present themselves favourably to the bulk of the population. They have many misconceptions, but their main reason is the fact that the banks ask for security which they do not have.

In spite of their ignorance about borrowing from the banks, most of the group members are in close contact with them. Over 80% of the members interviewed during this study had their own personal bank accounts. About 60% had opened their accounts before 1992, and none of their groups had been linked to K-Rep at that time. The remaining 40% who had opened their accounts since 1992 were all members of groups which were linked to K-Rep, and three quarters of them opened their accounts after the link was started. About 85% of the members had savings accounts, while the rest had current accounts because they needed a cheque facility.

This shows that most On-Lending Group members were quite well-off even before they started to benefit from K-Rep's finance, and that most people who do not have bank accounts when their groups are linked to K-Rep soon open them. Members are encouraged to open accounts to enable them to deposit their loan money and also to make their individual savings. Earlier experience also showed that when every member has a bank account it is easier to avoid manipulation by group leaders during loan disbursements, and it also avoids the security problems associated with cash disbursements. Each group is encouraged to open a current account through which loan funds are remitted. The members are then given personal cheques which they can pay into their own accounts. Every group was operating at least one account, although some had as many as three. Although none of the On-Lending Groups had borrowed from the banks, they were already good customers and the officers at least, were no strangers to dealing with banks.

About two-thirds of the On-Lending Groups had accounts with Barclays or Kenya Commercial Bank, because these two have by far the widest branch networks in Kenya. Only 5% banked with the Cooperative Bank, in spite of its traditional links to group-based activities of rural people, and 8% chose to bank with the Post Office, presumably because of its more convenient location.

Although none of the On-Lending Groups had before this study approached any commercial bank for credit for the group, and the majority of the members had never approached a bank for a loan as individuals, a quarter of the members had applied for individual bank loans, and half of them had been approved. This shows that in spite of the majority opinion, banks can, and actually do, lend to some members of groups as individuals.

The eleven members from our sample who had taken bank loans had borrowed sums ranging from Kshs. 10,000 to Kshs. 450,000, or US$180 to US$820. Only one borrowed more than Kshs. 200,000, and the majority had taken less than Kshs. 50,000. All had repaid their loans at the time of these interviews.

Eight of the eleven borrowers had been required to provide collateral, while the others had used their existing savings as security. Most had paid interest rates which were well under the 35% charged by K-Rep to their groups, and their groups to them, but they had also had to meet other charges including transport and legal fee. In spite of the fact that a significant proportion of their fellow group members had successfully applied for bank loans, however, only 7% of the 75 members whom we interviewed planned in the future to approach a bank for credit facilities. Only two of the eleven members who had borrowed from a bank before, planned to approach a bank for another loan. Elijah Odinga of Yala Group said that he had guarantors as was required by Barclays Bank, while Esther Wambui of Kugiwa Group said that she has a good credit history with her bank having borrowed from it three times before.

Those who have borrowed from banks earlier, and are now reluctant to approach them again gave several reasons. Some said that the banks' interest rate is too high, although it is actually well below the rate charged by K-Rep. Others said that other requirements such as the provision of guarantors and title deeds as security were difficult to satisfy. Their reluctance was summed up by the comment of one respondent: "I am comfortable with the K-Rep arrangement. In a group, if you have difficulties in repaying a loan, the group members are willing to help you, but with banks, this friendliness is absent."

The following two case studies describe the experienes of two On-Lending Group members who did borrow from a bank.

Case 1: Geoffrey Vamba Vuti

Geoffrey is a member of Kyeni Kya Wendo Group. He has two businesses which he established in 1992; selling of cereals and transport. He has taken three loans from the National Industrial Credit Bank, which is the business lending arm of Barclays Bank of Kenya.

The loans were as follows:

1990	Ksh. 70,000
1992	Ksh. 600,000
1996	Ksh. 2.8 million

He said that to the best of his knowledge, the bank charged him an interest rate of 21% on all the three loans. For the first and second loans, he provided the title deed of his house in Nairobi as security. He used the first loan to buy 12 acres of land, and the second to establish his businesses. Geoffrey used the lorry that he bought with the third loan as security for it, and the vehicle is registered in the bank's name until the loan is fully repaid.

Geoffrey joined the Kyeni Kya Wendo Group in 1996 when he was already servicing his third bank loan. He received Kshs. 30,000, or US$ 545 out of K-Rep's loan to the group in 1996, and is repaying it at a 'flat' interest rate of 20%, which amounts to a "real" rate of approximately 35% on the declining balance. This was the rate which K-Rep was charging to On-Lending Groups at the time, and the group passed on the same rate to its members. Kyeni Kya Wendo does not give members loans from its own savings, so Geoffrey has not been able to borrow any more.

Geoffrey was not sure whether he was would approach a bank for another loan because he was still servicing the third loan.

Case 2: Esther Wambui

Esther Wambui joined the Kugiwa Group in 1986. She operates a veterinary shop which she established in 1993 and a timber workshop started in 1996.

She had taken four loans from Barclays Bank, Kerugoya branch:

1994	Ksh. 30,000
1995	Ksh. 50,000
1995	Ksh. 100,000
1996	Ksh. 100,000

Those were all short-term business loans, and Esther said she was able to repay them within periods as short as three months. She said that the bank charged her an interest rate of 21% on all the loans.

Esther had also borrowed twice from her group's own savings fund, at 10% "flat" annual interest:

1994   Ksh. 5,000
1995   Ksh. 5,000

She had also received three loans from K-Rep's loans to the group, at the rate of 20% "flat" interest:

1993   Ksh. 25,000
1995   Ksh. 50,000
1996   Ksh. 90,000

Esther plans to continue borrowing from the bank. She says that she can get short-term loans very quickly from her bank when she has unexpected business opportunities or problems. She has the necessary experience to deal with the bank, and she thinks that bank interest rates are not as high as most people tend to believe.

Although it might be ideal for the microfinance institutions to encourage their more successful On-Lending Groups to borrow from banks, the reality is that those groups are unwilling to be handed over to the banks if their financial needs can still be met by the MFIs. K-Rep would not want to be seen as a nursery for formal financial institutions, but there is nothing to stop those On-Lending Groups that wish to be "graduated" to bank loans. It is not K-Rep's policy to discourage them, but the record suggests that although a small number of individual members may graduate, the groups themselves will be most unlikely even to be able to access loans from banks.

This evidence suggests that although the banks in Kenya are reluctant to lend to On-Lending Groups, the groups are providing them with large numbers of new savings customers, some of whom are "graduating" to become individual borrowers as well. The banks may be quite right to leave the On-Lending Group business to the new grant or subsidy funded institutions, so long as these institutions are able to sustain their own survival and expansion from their internally-generated funds, or further donor funds. If they can, the banks will continue to reap the benefit of what is effectively a subsidised marketing service for themselves. If the new MFIs do not survive, or cannot expand, it may be necessary for the banks to make funds available to them, in order to continue their business development function which has been pioneered and is presently being carried out at donors' expense.

The banks and On-Lending (self-help) Groups in India

In India, on the other hand, the banks are under strong political pressure to undertake lending to self-help groups, and the heavily subsidised NABARD refinance gives them a generous spread which should be enough to cover their trans-action costs and the likely risks of loss, given the experience so far. Nevertheless, the majority of bank branches are still reluctant, and it is significant that the State Bank of India, the largest Indian bank, which is often seen by other banks as the leader, is not represented among the 31 branches of 22 different banks which had financed the groups covered in this study. NABARD itself, which has vigorously supported the programme of group linkage for some six years, with generously subsidised finance and training, accepts that NGOs and On-Lending Groups them-selves are having to form their own alternative financial institutions because the banks are so reluctant to become involved (NABARD, 1995, p.51).

MYRADA has had perhaps the longest experience of promoting On-Lending Groups, and attempting to link them to banks. It is suggested (Fernandes, 1992, p.65) that the following reasons may explain the reluctance of banks, particularly at the branch level, to become involved:

- Branch managers are not confident that their superiors will support them or give them credit for it.
- The average first loan to a group is Rs 10000; this is larger than most loans to individuals under poverty-alleviation programmes, but is still small.
- Groups often meet early in the morning or late at night; banks staff are reluc-tant to go to meetings outside their own office hours, particularly when they live some distance from their branches.
- Bankers try to control the ways the groups operate; NGOs and the groups themselves resist this.

Various other reasons have been suggested to explain branch bankers' reluc-tance. Some say that there is a shortage of good NGOs (NABARD, 1995, p.54). They would prefer to lend to them, rather than direct to the groups (Fernandes, 1992, p.35). Those who are willing to lend directly would still prefer to respond to requests from NGOs rather than having to take the initiative of searching for groups themselves (NABARD, 1995, p.35). Others are nervous about the groups and their own dependence on NGOs, or about their informal status and lack of security. Some of those who are willing to lend to NGOs find that the NGOs are reluctant to borrow, or that they too lack security. In general, they view these groups as small-scale and relatively unimportant objects of charity, and not as a serious business opportunity.

These reasons are typical symptoms of uncertainty and unwillingness to change. Banks are rightly conservative, and they are by no means the first industry which has been reluctant to adopt new distribution channels. This uncertainty is reflected not only in the attitudes and behaviour of branch mangers and their staff, but also by their superiors. The NABARD study in Orissa (Panda and Mishra, 1996, p. 51) found that Self-Help Group loans had to be approved by a manager at least one level above branch management, even if the amount of the loan was within the normal discretionary limit of the branch manager. Even if the motive for this was to keep senior management informed about progress in a field which they sup-ported, the additional paper work which was involved actually discouraged branch staff from taking an initiative about which they were in any case very nervous.

We attempted to gain an impression of bankers' attitudes to On-Lending Group financing. Because banks are large organisations, perceptions can vary at different levels of the hierarchy. Discussions with corporate office staff of Canara Bank showed that management does not regard groups as a serious business opportunity, but as social banking. The senior managers were also clear that their branch managers could not afford to spend their time and energy on forming and nurturing groups. They are however keen that their branch managers should consider linkages wherever an NGO has formed good groups, and they have instructed all their senior operational staff to look out for good NGOs in their area of operation and to instruct their managers to establish linkage with On-Lending Groups in such areas. They are prepared to finance any amount to these groups, provided they are functioning well and are supported by a reliable NGO.

The Canara Bank management were also wary about the large number of new NGOs and stressed the importance of ensuring their credentials. They were not in favour of bulk lending to NGOs but preferred to lend directly to groups. They regretted that there were very few rural branch managers who had the commitment to take up such challenging assignments such as financing of On-Lending Groups. Their Rural Service Volunteer (RSV) scheme where generous incentives were provided to encourage clerical staff to take up development work on a full-time basis did not get the response they had expected.

The management of the Cauvery Grameena Bank was very enthusiastic about On-Lending or Self-Help Groups. The bank was itself vigorously forming and financing groups. The Chairman of this bank is convinced that groups have a positive impact on branches which do business with them. The regular visits of the branch staff to the village for working with the groups has improved the business of the branch in general. The rate of growth of advances, deposits and recovery in Gundulpet taluka of Mysore district where the bank was promoting Self-Help Groups was higher than that of their branches in the neighbouring talukas.

The management of the Aligarh Grameen Bank has selected a number of branches to implement the group intermediation approach, and the branch manager of the Narauna branch of this bank was sure that in the coming years he would be able to adopt at least two villages where all loans would be routed through On-Lending Groups.

The Oriental Bank of Commerce (OBC) is implementing group intermediation projects in the form of Mahila Grameen Banks (Women's Village Bank) in the districts of Hanumangarh (Rajasthan) and Dehradun (U.P.). The results are encouraging and though the initiative has evoked a mixed response from both within and outside the bank, the management is very optimistic of the outcome. Their attitude can be summarised in the words of the general manager, who commented "I am not worried about criticism as the success of the Bangladesh Grameen Bank is born out of one such experiment." The project manager of the Mahila Grameen Bank Project of OBC argues in favour of forming the Bank as an independent subsidiary of OBC.

Branch managers had a wide variety of opinions about On-Lending Group financing, ranging from cynicism, to excited optimism. One example was the manager of Ittanahalli branch of Canara Bank in Mandya district. He was so excited about the Self-Help Group approach that he said that he would be happy if the bank could release him to work on a full-time basis with groups. Other managers of the same bank, however, felt that like many other earlier experiments in rural finance, the Self-Help Group was a fad which would fade away soon.

One RRB Branch Manager in Karnataka state thought that while the concept of lending to groups was a good one, perceptions at corporate level could make or mar it. He cited the shift in emphasis that had taken place in his bank when senior management changed. The earlier management encouraged large-scale formation and financing of groups, but the new management was more cautious in its approach.

The management of the commercial banks, by and large, viewed Self-Help Group financing as a sound proposition, provided the involvement of their branch managers was restricted only to financing. They were not keen for their branch managers to be involved in the laborious process of forming and nurturing groups. If a branch manager took the initiative and formed groups, without neglecting his other work, the management did not object, but they were not willing to provide any additional branch staff for this work. Commercial bank management felt strongly that group financing would always remain insignificant in the overall business of their branches, unless many more NGOs came forward to form and nurture groups in a big way.

RRB managers were more enthusiastic about Self-Help groups, perhaps because they have fewer alternatives and the rural poor are their natural constituency. If branch staff move out into villages to work with groups, whether in collaboration with NGOs or not, this can help to enhance the business of their branches, in respect of deposits, advances, and recoveries, and it is suggested that this can more than compensate for the cost incurred in the formation and nurturing of groups.

Banks and On-Lending Groups—Barclays and Kenya Commercial Bank

Three typical Kenyan On-Lending group members, whose groups were already borrowing from K-Rep, called on the Accra Road branch of Barclays Bank in order to find out about the possibility of their groups borrowing from the bank.

At the Barclays branch they were told that the bank would be willing to consider extending facilities to them as individuals or as a group, up to a Kshs. 30,000 (approximately US$ 545) per individual member of a group of 20 members. The repayment period would be three years, at an interest rate of 28% per annum.

The loans would have to be secured by title deeds or lease certificates for land, or by share certificates. Individuals could also take loans of up to Kshs. 5000 or US$90, but they would have to be existing savings account holders. Since the bank insists on a minimum balance of Kshs. 5,000 in savings accounts, such loans would actually be fully secured.

Three other group members went the Eastlands branch of Kenya Commercial Bank. They were told that the Bank does not normally give loans to groups, and that applications of this sort were referred to the Bank's Special Loans Unit at Head Office. The officer emphasised that no loans are ever given without adequate security arrangements, and that any loan to a group would need to be guaranteed by a third party. The group would also have to have operated an account with the bank for not less than six months.

Conclusion

The responses of the two branches in Kenya show that these two banks are not willing to deal with On-Lending Groups in the way in which K-Rep and the other microfinance NGOs are doing. The security requirement effectively disqualifies the poorer people or their groups from borrowing, and it is clear that the major banks in Kenya, like those in most other countries, still look for total security for their smaller loans.

Most bankers in India and in Kenya seem to take a similar and rather negative view of On-Lending Group financing. A few branch managers have taken the initiative to identify or even to form groups themselves, but these seem to be rare examples of unusual commitment rather than models which management should expect others to follow. The Indian banks are generally taking a reactive rather than a proactive view; they will finance groups if suitable candidates are presented to them by competent NGOs, but will not themselves market their services to groups.

Some of the Indian Regional Rural Banks (RRB) may be an exception. There are 196 such banks, which were established during the 1980s in an effort to bring financial services to the poor in rural areas. Most of them are now technically bankrupt, mainly because they were only allowed to take on business which was fundamentally unprofitable. The RRBs are now being restructured. Most of the restrictions on their activity have now been lifted, and they actually have more freedom than the commercial banks in some areas, such as setting interest rates. Some of these banks, including the Dhenkenal, Cauvery and Aligarh Banks which were part of this study, are searching aggressively for new market niches. Under present circumstances, it appears that these RRBs may be the only banks which are likely to accelerate the pace of On-Lending Group linkage in India in a significant way.

The Kenyan banks are benefiting from the groups' own group deposits, and from the new accounts which their members are opening, but they do not appear to regard even the best groups as potential loan recipients themselves. For them, groups are a direct and indirect source of deposits, and a "school" from which some good individual loan customers can emerge. There seems to be little chance that any of them will move aggressively into this market in the foreseeable future.

It is unlikely that any Indian NGOs will on their own be able to "drag" the banks into this market, since those of them which have the capacity and interest are more likely to become financial intermediaries themselves, as K-Rep have done. Some banks are willing to finance them for this purpose, but the spread which is available is too small to cover even a small part of the cost. Funds are available from local and from international sources which may be cheaper and which are not tied to a specific on-lending rate. NGOs are more likely to choose these sources, and to develop as competitors rather than customers or intermediaries for the banks.

5.2.   Do On-Lending Groups Need the Banks ?

Before condemning or regretting the banks' general lack of enthusiasm for this new market, we should ask whether On-Lending Groups really need the banks, or indeed any other source of outside finance. Will they not eventually accumulate their own resources and evolve into quite new financial institutions ? Do their members really need savings facilities rather than credit, so that groups, or groups of groups, will be able to mobilise enough from their own members to satisfy their needs ? Peoples' absorption capacity expands with their wealth; when group members need and are able to make use of more substantial sums than their groups can mobilise from within, will they not be ready to "graduate" as some have in Kènya, and borrow individually from the banks ?

This study has concentrated thus far on ways in which On-Lending Groups can be used to channel loans to poorer borrowers; savings have been treated mainly as one form of partial security. It has already been pointed out, however, that these clients may need accessible savings facilities as much or more than they need to borrow. How effectively are the banks satisfying this need ?

It is easy to characterise traditional commercial banks as institutions which mobilise savings from the rural poor in order to lend them to the urban rich, but the major banks in Kenya appear to have turned their backs on small customers' savings as well as their loans. Table 23 lists the approximate minimum amounts which are required to open a savings account, and the minimum balance on which interest will be paid, for a number of banks in Kenya. It also gives the monthly penalty which some banks levy on accounts when the balance falls below the required minimum.

Table 23: Minimum Balances for Savings Accounts, Kenya and India

Bank	Minimum to open	Minimum for interest	Monthly penalty
Kenya Commercial Bank	$ 9	$ 118	$ 1.35
Barclays Bank of Kenya	$ 55	$ 90	–
Cooperative Bank of Kenya	$ 36	$ 109	$ 1
Standard Chartered Bank	$ 136	$ 180	$ 2
Banks in India	$ 6	$ 6	–

Note: These figures were obtained in November 1997, the US$ conversions are approximate.

The banks in India are not free to vary their minimum balance requirement without authority from the Reserve Bank, and it is unlikely that this regulation will be removed in the near future.

Most On-Lending Group members, even in India and certainly in Kenya, would find these minimum opening figures difficult, if not impossible, to reach. Even if they could open the accounts, they would certainly find it necessary to draw down their balances below the minimum interest-bearing levels from time to time. This would mean they would get no return on their money, and if they were unfortunate enough to fall to the penalty level, they would find that their savings being eroded not only by inflation but by the bank's charges.

These minimum balances are presumably set because the administrative cost to the banks of maintaining the accounts exceeds the earnings that can be made from the amounts deposited. The intention here is not to promote "socially responsible" but unprofitable behaviour, in lending or in deposit mobilisation. On-Lending Groups, however, can on-lend from their members to the banks as well as from banks to their members; their intermediation function operates in both directions.

If banks neglect the opportunity to take deposits from On-Lending Groups, and to lend to them, however, the groups will be forced to carry out their own intermediation functions, by developing multi-tier structures, as is already happening in India and elsewhere.

This is of course how financial institutions have generally evolved; subsidised assistance for micro-finance is no more than an attempt to "jump start" the process of capital accumulation. There is some evidence from various parts of the "developing" world that there really is no need for outside finance, on commercial or subsidised terms; all that may be needed is effective institutions. Geertz (1962) takes a sociological rather than a business or banking view of the future of ROSCAs, and suggests that they will evolve into banks or other new forms of financial institution, rather than being linked with them.

In northern Pakistan between 1984 and 1994 AKRSP promoted 1788 men's village organisations and 728 women's organisations, with a total membership of almost 100,000 people. They had accumulated Rs. 190 million, or almost five million dollars in savings, and had made loans to an accumulated total of approaching twice that amount, without any extra outside funding. The groups were initiated with the help of grants for infrastructure such as roads or bridges, and technical advice and training was provided free of charge, but the lending funds were entirely self-generated.

There was an element of subsidy in that the groups' savings were actually deposited in a commercial bank and then effectively re-borrowed from AKRSP at a slightly lower rate of interest, but this nevertheless demonstrates that very poor people can accumulate sufficient funds for their own needs within a fairly short period. Some groups had more funds than they needed at some times of year, while others had less; although AKRSP in no way promoted any form of higher level intermediation or wholesale intermediation between the very scattered and remote villages, some inter-group lending was taking place in 1994 and some group managers were discussing the idea of forming a People's Bank to facilitate this process (Harper A, 1995, p.45).

In Zimbabwe, there is a network of 500 women's savings and loan clubs which is apparently able to satisfy all its members' credit needs without any access to outside money (Fong and Perrett, 1991, p.49), and the Country Women's Association of Nigeria has developed a similar approach to banking in 720 villages with 78,600 women. They found that 'western' style institutions were not appropriate for their needs, and evolved new structures, again without any outside money (Ogunleye, 1996). In Francophone West Africa, also, it has been suggested that the women's On-Lending Groups, or Tontines, do not want or need linkages to the banks (Balkenhol, 1993). They require a quite different form of organisation, built on their own resources.

In the Indian temple city of Tirupati in Andhra Pradesh, a federation of women's On-Lending Groups have built up a fund of over $100,000, of which less than 10% has come from outside sources (Raghini, 1995, pp.25-26). The Co-operative Development Foundation (CDF), based in Hyderabad in India, has vigorously supported the cause of genuine cooperation, free of government interference. One way of doing this is to develop financial institutions with no outside money; CDF has, among other activities, promoted some 12,000 groups, with a membership of almost a quarter of a million women. These groups have accumulated well over one million dollars worth of savings, without any recourse to loan or grant funds from any source, and they are rapidly building a substantial new financial institution.

All these initiatives are of course very similar to the credit union or co-operative approach to financial intermediation. They, and many of the recent microfinance initiatives, are genuine cooperative endeavours, and it is a measure of the failure of the cooperative movement worldwide that the so-called "new generation" of institutions has come up outside the cooperative framework. Sadly, however, most cooperatives have been hijacked by political and other special interests, so that they have failed to be an effective vehicle for the equitable provision of financial or other services to poorer communities. It may be that the new institutions will be embraced by reformed cooperative movements, or will themselves for the basis for quite new movements. (NABARD-APRACA, 1996, p.97).

Regardless of their institutional form, however, there is also a strong body of evidence to suggest that although On-Lending Groups and their equivalents may establish multi-tier financial structures, as some already have, they will still need to access external finance in addition to their members' own resources if they are to satisfy their needs.

Although Village Banks have been established in many different countries, none of them has apparently yet attained financial self-sufficiency; they still need loans from their sponsors, because their members need more money than their fellows can save, and the whole system does not mobilise sufficient finance to satisfy them (Holt, 1994, p.179).

PRADAN promoted second- and third-tier organisations in Tamil Nadu, but found that these are complementary rather than competitive to the banks. Their main function is to provide small sums to their groups for their members' immediate needs. Larger sums are beyond their capacity. As the market for petty trading and other high return fast turnover micro-enterprises becomes saturated, the group members will need larger, longer-term finance for more substantial activities (Harper M, 1998, p.160). If the banks are ready to respond, the On-Lending Group members will be their customers of the future. Mayoux also found that silk reelers in southern India needed to be able to access outside capital. They could not raise the money they needed for capital equipment through their own groups (Ardener and Burman, 1995, p.192).

Organisations such as PRADAN, SEWA, or the Cooperative Development Foundation are promoting or developing new multi-tier financial structures not because their groups and their members do not need outside finance, but because the banking system is so insensitive to their needs, or even patronises and destroys them (Harper M, 1997, p.40). One major weakness of credit unions is the low rates of interest they charge, which prevents them from accessing the outside funds their members really need (GEMINI, 1995). On-Lending Groups generally charge high rates of interest, since their members are used to paying extortionate rates to moneylenders. This enables them in turn to pay the market rate or above for funds from formal institutions. If the banks are still unwilling or unable to respond to their needs, the only alternative is to build new alternative structures.

The sustainability of On-Lending Groups

K-Rep's original initiative with group loans aimed to promote group owned and managed enterprises. K-Rep "discovered" the merry-go-round type of groups while working with community based enterprises. These ROSCAs and other business associations such as "Jua Kali Associations" were mainly established to assist the enterprises that their members own and operate. When K-Rep realised the potential of these groups as financial intermediaries, they re-directed their programme towards them. The overall objective of K-Rep's intervention was to provide credit and savings services to the poor entrepreneurs who are members of the groups; this would in turn create jobs and increase incomes.

Organisations such as K-Rep may aim themselves to develop into full-service banking institutions which will serve their groups and their members in the future. Another purpose, however, may be to encourage On-Lending Group members to develop the habit of regular saving in order to enable them to do without K-Rep in the future. They will in time build a fund which they can not only use as security for K-Rep loans but may in the future use as a capital asset to on-lend to their members if and when K-Reps' funds are no longer available.

The On-Lending Groups were also expected to collect service charges and fees in order to boost their capital base. K-Rep makes a service or interest charge on its loans to groups at a rate of 35% on the declining balance, which is more or less the same as a 20% "flat rate". Each group in its turn was originally expected to charge its members at a "flat" rate of between 25–30% p.a. This would have ensured that the groups made a substantial profit on every loan that they gave to their members. It was thus envisaged that the groups would eventually build their own funds.

In actual fact, however, On-Lending Groups are indeed saving substantial sums, but they are not following K-Rep's advice to add a margin on to the cost of the loans they make to their members, over and above the 35% charge levied by K-Rep. None of the groups which was interviewed in this study required their members to pay any additional interest charge. The members said that if they had had to pay more than 35%, most of them would not be able to service their loans. CARE Kenya recommend that their groups should add 5% to the interest they pay to CARE when on-lending to their members; these groups are generally dealing with smaller amounts, and CARE itself charges a lower rate than K-Rep, so this approach may be more feasible in their case.

When they are lending from their own savings funds, the K-Rep groups only charge interest at a flat rate of 10%, or the equivalent of between 15% and 20% on the declining balance. This rate is barely enough to cover the decline in the value of money due to inflation, and the sums involved are in any case insufficient for interest at this level to make a significant contribution to the growth of the groups' funds.

Although K-Rep's On-Lending Groups generally do not make a surplus on their interest charges, the members usually agree to make a small payment, such as Ksh. 20, or about fifty cents, at every meeting to cover administrative costs. This pays for accounts books, travel costs and allowances for trips to the bank and similar items. These payments are too small to make any significant contribution to the group's lending fund, but they do prevent the fund from being eroded by administrative costs.

The groups seem nevertheless to have found another way of accumulating funds. Their members may be reluctant to pay what seem to be excessive rates of interest, but they are happy to make additional savings contributions to funds such as an "emergency" fund. These funds, whatever their name, contribute to the growth of the group's assets, and can be lent out or used for any other purpose on which the members may agree in case of need. In terms of members' cash flow and the groups' capital accumulation, these contributions are no different from higher rates of interest.

K-Rep's own staff, and representatives of other microfinance institutions such as KWFT and Faulu Kenya also believe that some On-Lending Groups can become self-sustaining, so long as they can overcome the problem of defaulters. As it is now, some K-Rep groups such as Ngwihoke Wihoke and Thika Gwikuria which had built a large savings base have had to use all their money to repay their loans; this obviously reduces their chances of attaining sustainability.

On-Lending Groups such as Kugiwa in Kirinyaga which has mobilised Kshs. 239,000 (equivalent to US$4,350), Wanyua in Thika (Kshs. 227,000—US$4,130) and Mitumba in Nyahururu (Kshs. 165,000—US$3,000) are still continuing to increase their assets. If they can avoid defaults, they will soon be able to sustain themselves without further loans from K-Rep. Kenya Women Finance Trust (KWFT) indicated that they have some groups that have already mobilised enough savings to sustain their continued on-lending. Table 24 shows that most groups are mobilising large volumes of savings and are at the same time covering their expenses from other income. Even the weakest groups are more than covering their expenses with their income and monthly savings, so that their funds are continuing to grow.

Table 24: Kenya: Monthly Savings, Income and Expenditure of On-Lending Groups

Variable	Mean	Minimum	Maximum	N
Savings to date	Ksh. 93,465.19	Ksh. 0	Ksh. 239,887	15
Monthly savings	4,372.73	1,000	15,800	11
Monthly income from other activities	8,583.33	1,000	16,800	6
Monthly expenses	7,001.67	10	16,800	6

Despite the fact that some groups appear to be proceeding towards sustainability, they all continue to depend on institutional finance. Not a single group which has been financed by K-Rep or any of the other micro-finance institutions has stopped borrowing from outside and decided to rely only on its own funds. Even groups which had received loans in excess of Kshs. 2 million (US$36,000), were still looking forward to their next loan. It appears that the demand for credit increases with access. All the groups which participated in this study, including those which are already into their third K-Rep loan, said that they intend to continue borrowing from K-Rep.

KWFT agreed that a given On-Lending Group's demand for credit increases the longer it is within their programme, and CARE Kenya pointed out that the risk of default also increases as the groups borrow larger sums. They are often very efficient in dealing with their first loans, hoping to get bigger loans after having successfully repaid, but after they have got the bigger loans, they then relax and defaults increase which destroy their chances of attaining sustainability. Microfinance institutions are already introducing stricter controls to avoid this problem, such as making members sign affidavits so that their debts to their groups are legally enforceable.

Approximate balance sheets were obtained for a sample of 18 On-Lending Groups in India, and two in Kenya, in order to assess what proportion of their total funds they have accumulated from their members' savings, and from their surplus on operations, as opposed to borrowing from outside. The consolidated figures can be summarised as given in Table 25.

Table 25: Comparative Financial Structure of Indian and Kenyan On-Lending Groups

	Indian groups		Kenyan groups	
Total funds of which:	Rs.	386,000(100%)	Ksh.	1,215,000(100%)
Members' savings	Rs.	126,000 (33%)	Ksh.	292,000(24%)
Retained surplus	Rs.	66,000 (17%)	Ksh.	7,000 (1%)
Loans from bank/K-Rep	Rs.	193,000 (50%)	Ksh.	916,000(75%)

These figures show that the Indian banks' demand for On-Lending Groups to have savings equal to half or even the whole of the initial amounts they wish to borrow has encouraged their members to contribute a far higher share of their On-Lending Groups' funds than the Kenyans. K-Rep requires that the groups should have savings only of 10% of the amounts they borrow; their accumulated savings are well over this amount, but they are still contributing only half as much of their groups' funds as the Indian members.

The higher proportion contributed from the Indian On-Lending Group's surplus is presumably also caused in part by their higher proportion of members' funds, which they can lend out at interest but for which the group does not have to pay. The Indian Self-Help Groups are also benefiting from the lower rate of interest they have to pay for their loans from the banks. They pay 12% as opposed to K-Rep's effective rate of 35%, and can therefore add on a substantial spread when they on-lend to their members. The banks in India can only afford this low rate because they in their turn can refinance their group loans at the heavily subsidised rate of 6.5%.

Do On-Lending Groups need Banks ?—The Ma Bhuasini Women's Group

Whenever the lower caste women of Talasahi hamlet in Karadapalli Village in Orissa had an urgent need for money they had no alternative but to borrow from moneylenders, who charged very high rates of interest. They therefore agreed to follow the advice of a field worker from Adhikar, a local NGO, when he suggested that they might start a savings group.

They started with sixteen members, and five more joined later. They started saving in June 1996; they agreed that each member should save a minimum of Rs. 5 a week, or about fourteen cents, and that there would be no maximum. They also continued their traditional practice of contributing one handful of rice each every week. They opened a savings account at a nearby branch of a commercial bank, but they do not use it very much because their money is usually lent out to the members or held in cash for use in the near future.

The group charges its members 5% a month for their loans, which is less than they used to pay the moneylenders. The loans are for a maximum of three months, and each member has to persuade two others to guarantee her loan. The whole group discusses every application, and the loans are only disbursed on Sundays, at their regular meetings. They have agreed, however, that in cases of emergency the committee can make immediate decisions and disbursements. All the loans are for their own individual purposes, but at harvest time, they collected their whole fund and bought raw paddy from the local market. They processed this and sold it, and contributed the profit of Rs. 1600 to the group's fund.

By February 1997 the group had accumulated almost Rs. 10,000. Their savings amounted to just over Rs. 7,150, and in addition to the Rs. 1,600 profit from the paddy processing they had earned almost Rs. 1,000 from the interest they had paid on their loans. The bank had paid them Rs. 66 interest on their savings account, but they were agreed that they had better ways of using their money than leaving it in the bank. They had all benefited individually from the loans they had taken, and they also realised that they had in only nine months been able to accumulate a group fund worth one-and-a-half times what they had saved. They seemed to be able to build their own fund without any need to borrow from anyone else.

Conclusion

The weight of the evidence, from these studies and from other sources, suggests that most, but by no means all On-Lending Groups will continue to need to borrow from outside sources, and that their own savings and accumulated surplus will not be sufficient. Some members who can make effective use of large sums may "graduate" and become individual bank customers, but they may also wish to remain within their groups and to borrow through them as well.

NGOs are promoting new and independent multi-tier financial structures, or are converting themselves into "new generation" financial institutions, not because the On-Lending Groups will be able eventually to fund their own needs, but because the existing commercial banks are generally unwilling to deal with them, particularly at the branch level. Higher level entities, such as PRADAN's Federations which represent clusters of groups, can bypass the bank branches and access funds at a higher level and from different institutions.

As this trend continues, and the new institutions are licensed to take deposits, the banks will find that On-Lending Groups' savings are no longer deposited with them. Their members will lose whatever contact they now have with their local banks, and will bring increasing pressure on the new institutions to offer individual banking services. In time, therefore, the new institutions can be expected to evolve into full-service banks, which have close links with the mass of the population. If the existing commercial banks wish to abdicate from mass market retail banking in poorer rural and urban areas, this will be no problem, but if they wish to retain and strengthen their national coverage they should as a matter of urgency reconsider their policy towards this kind of groups.

CHAPTER 6

CONCLUSIONS AND RECOMMENDATIONS

An attempt has been made to answer certain specific questions in the foregoing chapters. Readers must judge for themselves from the evidence presented whether the questions have all been satisfactorily addressed, and what are the answers.

The questions are repeated here, and each is followed by a summary of the findings, with some suggestions as to what the findings imply for bankers, and NGO staff, who work in this field.

Questions about the groups and their members

> Are there large numbers of potential groups in most communities, already involved in some sort of cash or in-kind saving and lending, and if there are, how easy is it for them to evolve into suitable banking intermediaries ?

Group activity is everywhere. Informal group financial intermediation through ROSCAs is very common in some communities, but is by no means universal. People who have been members of ROSCAs are familiar with handling money that belongs to the group, and are used to the idea that intermediation necessarily requires some members to wait longer than others, and in effect to save, while others borrow.

ROSCAs do not, however require a long-term commitment, and it may be easier to build On-Lending Groups on the foundation of non-monetary group activities, where people have been used to working together for a common end over a long period.

Some ROSCAs, however, have been in existence for many years, and some have also gone beyond the simple cycle of collection and disbursement of the total "pot". They are already engaged in accumulating and lending larger sums, in charging interest and in dealing with recoveries and defaulters. It is not difficult for these groups to manage outside finance.

Branch bankers should in any case be close to the communities they serve, and should be alert for any distribution channel through which they can profitably reach new customers. They should be aware of the existing level and types of group activity and informal intermediation, and be ready to offer savings and lending products which are appropriate for local circumstances.

Marketing to this new distribution channel may involve training or community development skills. If these go beyond what the banker has or is prepared to offer, he should also be familiar with any NGOs which operate in his area. They may be happy to undertake the necessary work, in the knowledge that they will thereby be linking their clients to new sources of finance.

Are the poor (meaning the poorest who can benefit from loans, and repay without hardship) members of such groups ?

The poorest people in a given community are not usually members of On-Lending Groups. They are excluded by other people in the community, because they do not want to take the risk of covering their defaults. They are self-excluded, because they doubt their own ability to save or to make profitable investments. They are also excluded by NGOs because their inclusion can weaken the social and financial cohesion of the group. This exclusion may be in their best interest, since borrowing necessarily involves the possibility of loss. The poorest people are those who can least afford to lose what little they have.

This does not mean, however, that very poor people cannot be members of and benefit from On-Lending Groups. In India in particular, and to a lesser extent in Kenya and elsewhere, the poorest people tend to live in their own separate communities. These may be within a village or slum, and the poorest people may play a vital part in the wider community, such as scavenging or providing casual labour, but they are separate in a social sense. They have their own groups, on the basis of which On-Lending Groups have been built, and every member of such a group will be poor.

The poorest within the poor community, sometimes known as "the poorest of the poor", probably will be excluded, but On-Lending Groups are not a "quick fix" or automatic cure for poverty. The group members are, however, poor people, and they generally live in the same communities as the poorest. If the slightly better-off inhibitant of a particular rural village or urban slum are able to become a little less poor some part of their greater prosperity can be expected to "trickle down" to their poorer neighbours.

Poor communities are therefore a fruitful ground in which On-Lending Groups can flourish, and from which some people can "graduate" from poverty. The Indian groups appear to reach poorer people more effectively than those in Kenya, perhaps because most of them have been promoted by NGOs with a concern to alleviate poverty, rather than being formed by their own members without any external influence other than the possible availability of finance. Promoters of On-Lending Groups should not, however, try to force members to include the poorer people if they wish to exclude them. Bankers should be aware of the potential of poor people's groups to mobilise savings, and eventually to make effective use of additional finance.

> Can a group function with no literate members and no routine outside help, or must an NGO person or other literate outsider always act as manager or secretary ?

On-Lending Groups need written records of some kind, in a way that an independent business owned by one person may not, because all the members need to be able to know how they stand within the group, and the financial position of the group as a whole. This does not mean, however, that they must have a fully trained bookkeeper, or even a member with secondary education. There are indeed some dangers in having one or two members with much higher education than the rest, since homogeneity is important for effective group cohesion, and an educated minority may be tempted to use their position to deceive the less fortunate fellow-members.

Literacy is a matter of degree, and a great deal depends on the kind of records which have to be kept. NGOs and banks can force groups to be dependent on themselves, or on other outsiders, if they demand that they maintain unnecessarily complex systems.

On-Lending Groups can also be the means whereby their members acquire the skills they need. Most illiterate people want to learn to read and write, and some form of group organisation is necessary for adult literacy training. If members learn as well as save together, the group will be stronger for both purposes, and NGOs can achieve educational as well as economic goals at the same time.

Outside assistance may be necessary for some time but it is important that the group remains in charge of its own affairs, even if the records are being maintained by someone who is not a member. If the group pays for the bookkeeping service, this can contribute towards an effective relationship.

> Do the loans and their repayment genuinely benefit all members, so that they are better-off than before ?

People do not have to become members of On-Lending Groups, or to remain indefinitely as members. But the best evidence that someone is benefiting from membership is probably the fact that she is still a member. Nevertheless, social pressure may force some members to remain in when they would rather leave, or the terms under which savings and the share of accumulated profits are refunded to those who leave may also discourage resignations, as indeed they are intended to do. It is therefore right to "second guess" members' decisions, and to check how equitably the benefits of membership are shared within the group.

The evidence shows that most members do benefit, but that the better-off, including the leadership, benefit more than the others, proportionately and in absolute terms. This is only to be expected, since the richer people have more opportunities for investment, and skills to exploit them, and they can also afford to take larger risks than the poor. If the poorer members do not actually lose by their membership, we should be content.

On-Lending Groups are micro-banks, owned and managed by their customer members. If bankers who lend money to them, or NGOs which promote them, become too involved in their management they will subvert the very autonomy and independence which are their main merits. Gross exploitation by the better-off members will almost certainly lead to break-up of a group, and non-repayment of loans from outside. Lenders should therefore be aware of this danger, but they neither need nor should try to impose or even encourage equity in the allocation of loans which goes beyond what the members themselves want.

> What proportion of members default or drop out, and are they as a result of this worse off than before ?

It appears that between 10% and 20% of On-Lending Group members drop out of the groups for one reason or another. Some may "graduate", and leave because they no longer need the services the group provides—they have no need for further credit, or they can access finance more conveniently, and less expensively, from other sources. Others may drop out because they find the requirements of membership too demanding; the demand for regular savings may be beyond their wishes or capacity, or they may not have time to attend meetings.

This is not necessarily a sign of misfortune; some people find working in and with groups more acceptable than others. Yet others drop out because they cannot repay their loans on time. The group may have recovered their money through sale of pledged assets or by other means, or it may have been necessary for their fellow members to make good the losses from their own savings. In either case, they were expelled.

Those who drop out because of business problems are clearly worse off than they would have been if they did not have such problems, but their misfortune has not necessarily been caused by their membership of a group. Banks are sometimes blamed for the failure of their business clients; this is usually because they are perceived to have been insensitive to the realities of the enterprise and have "pulled the plug" too early. Less frequently, they are blamed for having encouraged clients to invest in unviable ventures, or those that were beyond their management capacity.

There is no evidence to suggest that On-Lending Groups have been responsible for their members' business failure in either way. A business-woman's fellow members in a group are almost certainly better able than any banker to judge whether she is capable of managing the business she wishes to expand or set up with her loan, or whether they can safely allow her some leeway in repayment in order to tide over a temporary problem.

It can probable be concluded with confidence that On-Lending Groups do less damage to their members than banks. By using groups as an intermediary, a bank can not only reduce its transaction costs and attain a higher level of repayment, but it can also mitigate the hardship that business difficulties cause to their owners, anywhere.

Questions about the use of groups for financial intermediation

Does outside money "spoil" the groups, reduce their motivation, or demand too much of their management ?

Outside money of course makes new demands on an On-Lending Group, and of its member's capacity to make good use of it. Like any additional resource, it constitutes a challenge; a strong group can use it to become stronger, but a weak group may be destroyed by it.

The amount of money, and above all its timing, are critical. If a group has only been a savings group, and has not proceeded to the stage of lending from its own fund, it is less likely to be able to cope with the twin challenges of the new money and the quite new type of activity. A ROSCA is a savings and lending operation in a way that a group whose members only make savings is not, but its management requires few decisions and no records apart from a list of which members have taken the 'pot' so far. This need not even be written.

Much has been made of the distinction between "hot" money, which is people's own money which they have saved or earned, and "cold" money which has been provided by someone else. People are naturally less inclined to use "cold" money effectively, to make records of it, or to repay it. Grants are clearly cold, and so are loans which are given at low rates of interest under some special "scheme", particularly when everybody knows that most people do not repay them and do not suffer in consequence. A number of NGOs which at one time used grants as a means of encouraging On-Lending Groups have stopped. Quite apart from the cost, they have found that it was not a productive way of promoting group autonomy.

Money which is borrowed from a commercial bank, or from a NGO which is known to behave like a bank, at the same rates of interest which other borrowers pay for similar amounts on similar terms, is surely hot, or at least a great deal warmer than grants. If a bank is willing to lend to an On-Lending Group like any other customer, this in itself constitutes a statement that the members are not "weaker sections" in need of special concessions, but are responsible people who can be dealt with on mutually profitable terms like any customer. Individuals, and groups, behave as they believe they will be expected to behave.

Financial intermediation requires specialisation, and outside money can have the effect of diverting On-Lending Group members' interest from other social activities which may have been the original reason for which the group was formed. This may be the price which has to be paid for economic progress, and the poorer members may lose more than the better-off as a result. On-Lending Groups are not a panacea or even a mainline remedy for poverty, and there must still be room for charity.

> How can On-Lending Groups be developed most effectively and brought to the level required for borrowing from banks ? How long does this process take ?

The process of group development has been widely covered elsewhere, and the principles are no different for On-Lending Groups than for any other group. The most effective groups are those where the initiative came from within, and where no outside "promoter" was involved at any stage.

Organisations which wish to develop these groups must recognise that there are probably nascent or even fully developed groups within the community already, and it is quicker, and in the long-term more effective, to build on what already exists. They should also remember that the process of "storming" seems to be a vital part of group development, and if some members leave at an early stage as a result of conflicts this is probably a positive sign.

Group promoters must err on the side of doing too little rather than too much; this may be particularly important for the development of On-Lending Groups, which are moving towards becoming independent micro-banks. As with individual entrepreneurs, group promoters should not be afraid of failure; it is much less expensive, in social and financial terms and for all parties, if a group is judged not to be able to make use of a loan than if it gets one and is unable to deal with it successfully.

Groups should be set clear tasks, such as achieving certain levels of saving, or making certain decisions; if they fail, they can try again, but promoters must not be misled by their enthusiasm to make exceptions.

The time taken to 'develop' a group into an effective financial intermediary will obviously depend on the stage it had reached before the external 'developer' became involved. It is unlikely that any group would be ready to take a bank loan in much less than three months from the first contact by the NGO or bank branch, and two years is probably enough for any group where the potential exists at all, even if it has to start completely from "scratch".

> How can groups be assessed most efficiently ? What objective and other indicators can be used to judge that a group is a good intermediary ?

The appraisal of On-Lending Groups, like that of any loan applicants, involves a combination of objective and subjective indicators. There is no substitute for good judgement, and the ultimate decision cannot be reduced to a formula.

There are certain generally accepted indicators, however, which are agreed to be both useful and practical. They can be categorised into those which are objectively verifiable, and those which depend more on personal judgement.

The 'hard' indicators include:

- The group must be able to show that it has existed for at least one year
- All the members must have their own businesses, however small
- All the members must have been saving for at least one year
- The group must hold regular meetings, which are not postponed
- All the members must regularly attend the meetings
- The group must have some written records to substantiate the above
- The group should not have more than 30 members
- The group must want to borrow for individual, not for group business
- The group must be officially registered if this is practical
- The members must know how much their own savings are
- The group must have a bank account
- The group must already be making and recovering loans from its own fund

The "softer" and more subjective indicators include:

- The leadership must be effective, and should be rotated regularly
- The group must operate and make decisions in a democratic way
- The group must be able to operate independently of its promoters
- The group's membership must be homogeneous
- The group must demonstrate its "empowerment"
- The group must be independent of political interests

There is also some evidence that groups of women are better customers than men; mixed groups are inappropriate in some societies, but the record of all male groups is worse than that of all women's groups, everywhere.

Not all these indicators are appropriate in every situation, and some lenders may demand less. It is important, however, for On-Lending Groups to be as rigorously assessed as any loan applicant. Lenders must remember that if they make the wrong decision, they will injure not just one borrower but a large number of people, many of whom are very vulnerable.

> What is the cost of the group development and assessment tasks? Are these tasks most efficiently undertaken by a bank or by an NGO ?

Bankers may be discouraged from lending to groups because they are unfamiliar, and they fear that the costs of developing and assessing them will be so high that the relationship will never be profitable.

The management of many, if not most, rural bank branches in India and in Kenya would not be able to state what was the average cost of acquiring a new client, or of assessing a loan proposal, and it is thus difficult to compare On-Lending Groups with individual clients. It is also difficult to separate the costs of developing a group and of assessing it in order to decide whether it is ready to borrow and to repay outside finance.

There appears nevertheless to be a remarkable degree of consistency between the costs of On-Lending Group development, and assessment, as estimated in this study and as published by others. It costs about $200 to develop a group, and $20 to assess it. These simple figures beg many questions as to the condition of the group when the development process started, its size, its location and so on, but they do at least provide a basis of comparison on which bankers may be able to base a decision as to whether they should consider entering this market or not.

Indian rural bankers' previous experience of the kind of people who are members of these groups has generally been that of dealing with them under government sponsored "schemes" such as the Integrated Rural Development Programme (IRDP), which were characterised by massive defaults, high administrative costs and low returns. On-Lending Groups are preferable on all counts, but it was not possible to obtain a specific comparable figure for the cost of dealing with the same number of customers individually, or of dealing with one larger customer borrowing the same amount. Their continued reluctance to deal with On-Lending Groups appears, however, to be because of their unfamiliarity rather than because of any specific objections to the costs or the risks.

If a bank is going to lend to a group, the banker must of course assess it. The development task in India, however, has usually been carried out by a NGO, at no cost to the bank. In Kenya the On-Lending Groups have developed themselves, sometimes in response to the possibility of a loan from K-Rep. The Kenyan tradition of group-based financial intermediation is however much stronger than in India, partly perhaps because there have been fewer alternative sources of financial services for poorer people.

If a NGO is willing and able to develop On-Lending Groups, and to bring them as 'ready-made' customers to a bank for assessment and a possible loan, the banker would obviously be foolish to decline the service and to undertake the development himself. If there are no competent NGOs available, and a banker wishes to enter this market, he may have the choice of paying an NGO to come to the area, or of developing the groups himself as has been done in Pingua, Bommalapura and Ittanahali.

In spite of the success of these isolated cases, it is likely that most banks would find it less expensive and more effective to pay NGOs to develop groups for them than to do it themselves. NGO costs are lower and their 'culture' is more suited to community development, even with a strong financial content, than that of most banks. Some NGOs in India are already undertaking the development of individual enterprises for banks on a performance fee basis; if the same approach was adopted for On-Lending Groups, the whole bank linkage movement would be placed on a far more transparent and business-like footing.

> Can On-Lending Groups afford to pay interest rates which are high enough for their business to be profitable for the banks which lend to them ?

On-Lending Groups' ability to pay depends on what they can afford to charge their members for their loans; this in turn depends on what their members can afford. Investments in micro-enterprise yield very high returns, even when adjusted for the opportunity cost of the owner's labour; it is unusual for the annual return on the total sum invested, or even on investments in expanding the business, to be under 100%. Groups which have reached the level of borrowing outside funds only lend a small part of their portfolio for consumption purposes, and these loans are usually for small short-term amounts where interest rates are far less important than immediate access.

The interest charged on loans to On-Lending Groups by banks in India is kept artificially low because the loans can be refinanced at a heavily subsidised rate. Some institutions in India are already lending to groups at higher rates, however, and the rates charged by K-Rep and other micro-finance institutions in Kenya are as much as three times higher. These higher rates prevent the groups from adding a margin which is large enough to make a significant contribution to the rate at which they accumulate their own funds, but the members continue to borrow at these high rates, even those who can also borrow individually from banks.

Banks should therefore not be nervous about charging On-Lending Groups rates which are as high or higher than those charged to individual customers for the same amounts on the same terms. The appraisal, and certainly the development of groups involve extra costs, but these can be recovered over time from interest income. Banks in India whose cost of funds is below 12% might do well to consider lending to Groups at 18% or more without taking advantage of NABARD refinance. Their spread would be more than that allowed by NABARD, and this would also send the message that On-Lending Groups are not weak but are viable customers, who can afford to pay the same interest rates as any other borrowers.

> How can a group's own savings be used as security in ways which members will take seriously but which does not mean that they are effectively borrowing their own money ?

Bankers cannot expect On-Lending Groups to provide 100% tangible security. Their members may or may not have sufficient assets, but the forms in which they are held, and the costs of registration, title deeds and so on mean that they are not viable securities.

The repayment record of On-Lending Groups, however, and of their members to the groups, is generally such that any banker who is in any way open to taking less than 100% security will at least consider the possibility of financing them. The intangible pressure which group members exert on their fellows, in order to protect whatever security they have pledged and to preserve their own future ability to borrow, is often much more powerful than the threat of asset seizure is to an individual borrower, particularly if he is well aware that the asset in question is effectively inalienable.

Groups must learn to save before they can learn to borrow, and even in a simple ROSCA all the members except the one who draws the first "pot" are effectively saving before they borrow. This need to save can be the means whereby a group generates partial security, which may be 50% as is usual for first loans in India, or as low as 10% as required by K-Rep.

If twenty people each stand to lose a small amount, they can impose far more stringent sanctions on a single potential defaulter than a bank can ever do itself. Fifty per cent security, or even 10% , which is contributed by 20 people can generate more pressure than 100% which is contributed by one.

The lender must decide whether to accept evidence of the existence of the necessary savings, and to allow the On-Lending Group to continue to use the money for loans, or to require that it should be kept on deposit. The decision will depend in part on the proportion that is required, but some banks in India demand that 50% or even 100% or more of the outstanding balance should be held on deposit and mandated to the lender. NGOs and other observers claim that this is inequitable, but the groups themselves appear to accept it as the price of future loans.

What really stops banks from lending to On-Lending Groups ? Is it ignorance, on which side ? Is it because groups do not approach banks, because groups do not need loans from banks, because groups lack security or are not registered legal bodies or because assessing groups takes too long or is too difficult ?

The concept of bank lending to On-Lending Groups has been discussed for more than some ten years, and it has been vigorously promoted in India and elsewhere for about seven years. In Kenya K-Rep itself and other microfinance NGOs have effectively demonstrated that it is possible and profitable. In spite of the promotion, the training and the practical demonstration, however, the practice has not been adopted as part of any bank's mainstream lending activity, anywhere. Bankers may be conservative and cautious, but they are also anxious to identify new and profitable markets, as well as demonstrate their social commitment. Why have they not used On-Lending Group intermediation as a means to achieve both ends ?

There are many reasons for this reluctance, some which are based on fact and others which are misconceptions but are nevertheless equally important. Some of the misconceptions, particularly but not only at the branch management level, include:

- Group-based activities never work
- NGOs are anti-business and anti-bank
- Banks must deal direct with their customers, not through intermediaries
- Groups are not bank's business, NGOs or government should deal with them
- Groups cannot afford to pay bank interest rates
- People in my area do not work in groups

Other more soundly-based objections include:

- Subsidies have created expectations which make On-Lending Group linkage unprofitable
- Poor people have been spoilt by subsidy
- The legal status of On-Lending Groups is unclear
- Neither the groups nor their members can offer 100% security
- Banks cannot afford to risk being seen to seize poor people's savings
- New private institutions are taking up On-Lending Group business
- Groups do not have records which we can understand
- Groups need more follow-up
- Banks can profit from taking deposits from On-Lending Groups—there is no need to lend to them
- Bank staff are not willing to work with poor people
- Groups have to be dealt with outside office hours
- Bankers need new skills to deal with Groups
- There are not enough competent NGOs to develop On-Lending Groups
- Senior management do not support new initiatives
- The volume of business will not justify the effort

Each of these objections, and many others, must be examined. Many were true but are becoming less so, and some may in some cases be justified; it is not suggested that every commercial bank should at once enter whole-heartedly into On-Lending Group financing. The opportunity does however justify dispassionate appraisal. Support is available for training, but banks should not make use of these resources unless they are convinced that the actual banking transactions will be profitable. Half-hearted or subsidised attempts to enter this new market may only have the effect of discouraging others.

The evidence surely suggests that this is a major and profitable new market for many banks, particularly those with large under-used rural networks. One option may be total withdrawal from the poorer rural and urban markets, in order to focus on corporate business. Any bank which does not choose this route, however, must seriously examine On-Lending Groups.

> Will groups eventually build their own funds and no longer need outside money, or will their needs grow with their access, so they continue to borrow from the bank ?

On-Lending Groups can accumulate funds from their members' own savings or from whatever surplus they may earn as a result of their on-lending operations; this may be from the spread between the interest they pay and that they charge, or from fines or other charges they may choose to levy on themselves.

The groups in India and in Kenya continue to save even when they have received loans from outside. In Kenya their savings are usually earmarked as security for future loans rather than used directly for on-lending, but they still add to the group's own funds, providing of course that the group does not have to draw on them to cover defaults.

The Indian Self-Help Groups are accumulating their own funds more rapidly than the K-Rep financed groups in Kenya; they are making a large spread from their on-lending, and their default rate also appears to be lower. They pay a lower rate for their institutional loans, but their members are poorer than those in Kenya. They therefore need to borrow smaller sums and can afford to pay higher interest rates on them.

Whatever their rate of capital accumulation, however, the weight of the evidence suggests that group members' effective need for finance expands with their access, at a pace which exceeds the rate of increase of their own funds. As they become less poor, members acquire skills and are otherwise empowered to undertake larger, more capital-intensive enterprises, with a slower and lower rate of return than the petty trading and other short-term activities on which they previously relied. The issue, therefore, may not be whether On-Lending Groups need outside funds, but where they are going to obtain them.

Many Indian On-Lending Groups, and the NGOs which promote them, have felt compelled to look for alternative sources of finance because the obvious source, their local commercial bank, is unwilling even to consider their applications. Many Indian banks, in fact, still refuse even to take deposits from groups, and while the banks in Kenya are happy to take their deposits, and to collaborate with K-Rep and the other microfinance NGOs in the movement of funds, none of them has yet made a loan at its own risk with its own funds to an On-Lending Group.

In India, the groups are therefore building new multi-tier structures, which can access development finance from national or international sources. In Kenya the microfinance NGOs have already made a small but significant impact on this market, with no competition from the banks at all. K-Rep itself is becoming a commercial bank, and both NGOs and new financial institutions in India are also starting to recognise that On-Lending Groups may be profitable customers.

The market is thus being addressed from many directions, by client-owned institutions, by NGOs which may be converting themselves into banks or by new privately owned businesses. As has so often happened, this new market, and the new distribution channels through which the market can be reached, are being more enthusiastically and more profitably exploited by new institutions rather than by the existing "natural" suppliers.

Many questions remain unanswered, but in the long term the commercial banks may need On-Lending Groups and the business they can offer more than the groups will need the banks.

BIBLIOGRAPHY

Alila, PO, 1988. Rural Development in Kenya: A Review of Past Expereinces, Regional Development Dialogue, Vol. 2, Summer.

Ardener, S and Burman, S (eds.), 1995. Money-go-Rounds, Berg, Oxford.

ASA, 1996. Drop-out on Micro-credit operation, Association for Social Advancement (ASA), Dhaka.

Ashe, J, 1992. Microlending Programs, in Community Development Investing, Boston.

Bakhoum I et al. Banking the Unbankable, 1989. Panos London.

Balkenhol, B, 1993. Tontines and the banking system—is there a case for building linkages? ILO, Geneva.

Bank Poor '96, 1996. MicroFinance for the Poor, Bank Por, Kuala Lumpur.

Berenbach S, and Guzman, D, 1994. *The solidarity group experience worldwide*, in, Otero: M, and Rhyne, E.

Cashbank, 1993. GCC History written in 1993 after the GCC's change of direction, Cashbank, Cape Town, unpublished report, supplemented by personal communication.

Creditwatch, 1996. Marathwada, State level consultation, women and On-Lending Groups, SPARC, Mumbai.

Dixit, M, 1996. Report on exposure visit to Bank Indonesia's SHG Linkage programme, unpublished note, SDC, Delhi.

Fernandes, AP, 1992. The MYRADA Experience—Alternate Management System for savings and credit of the rural poor, MYRADA, Bangalore.

Fong, MS and Perrett, H, 1991. Women and Credit, Finafrica, Cariplo, Milan.

Foundation for Development Cooperation, 1992. Banking with the Poor, Brisbane.

Geertz, 1962. 'The Rotating Credit Association: a 'Middle rung' in development, in: Economic Development and Cultural Change, Vol. 10, No. 2, pp. 241-263.

Gemini, Microenterprise development brief 13, 1995. Credit Unions, a formal sector alternative for financing microenterprise, GEMINI, Bethesda.

Grameen Trust, 1997. Grameen Dialogue 31, Dhaka.

Harper, Annie, 1995. The Management of Community Credit and Savings Groups, EDC, Cranfield University, Cranfield.

Harper, M and Finnegan, G, 1998. Small Enterprise Development—Value for Money? Oxford & IBH, Delhi.

Harper, M, 1997. Self-help groups, some issues from India, Small Enterprise Development, Volume VII, No. 2.

Harper, M, 1998. Profit for the Poor, Oxford & IBH, New Delhi/IT Publications, London.

Holloh, D and Soejipto, M, 1991. Self-help Groups in PPHBK, Bank Indonesia Jakarta.

Holt, SL, 1994. The Village Bank Methodology. Performance and Prospects, in: Otero M. and Rhyne, E.

Hulme, D and Mosley, P, 1996. Finance against Poverty, Routledge, London.

Jayasundere, R, 1994. Savings and Credit, The selection of Loanees, IRED, Colombo.

Krishnamurthy, K, 1992. Self-Help Groups, experiment and experience, Paper presented at CAB Pune.

Magill, J, 1994. Credit Unions, in: Otero, M. and Rhyne, E.

Microcredit Summit, 1996. Draft Declaration, Washington, DC.

Montgomery, R, 1996. Disciplining or Protecting the Poor ? Avoiding the Social Costs of peer pressure in solidarity group micro-credit schemes, Paper presented at conference on Finance against Poverty, Reading.

Mutua, K, et al., 1996. It Did Not Happen Overnight, The history of group-based credit programmes in Kenya, K-Rep, Nairobi.

Mwaniki, R, et al., 1996. Chikola Credit Scheme: Policies and Procedures Manual, K-Rep Technical paper No. 14, Nairobi.

NABARD, 1995. Linking Self-Help Groups with Banks, Bombay.

NABARD-APRACA, 1996. International Seminar on development of the rural poor through Self-Help Groups, May 1995, Proceedings, NABARD, Mumbai.

Narender, K, 1996. Training Manual for Community Banking, Sri Padmavathy Mahila Abyudaya Sangam, Tirupati.

Ogunleye, B, 1996. Creating Wealth through Traditional Credit, International Agricultural Development.

Otero, M, and Rhyne, E. (eds.), 1994. The New World of Microenterprise Finance, Intermediate Technology Publications, London.

Otero, M, 1989. A Question of Impact, ASEPADE/PACT, Tegucigalpa.

Panda, AK and Mishra, AK, 1996. SHGs in Orissa, NABARD, Bhubaneswar.

PRADAN, 1996. Training material for exposure programme on Banking with SHGs, PRADAN/NABARD, Madurai.

Project on Linking Self-Help Groups with Banks, 1996. Status as on 31 March 1996, NABARD, Mumbai.

Pulzahendi, 1995. Transaction Costs of Lending to the Poor, Foundation for Development Co-operation, Brisbane.

Raghini, D, 1995. Community Banking—our Gurthimpu, Sri Padmavathy Mahila Abyudaya Sangam, Tirupati.

RBI and NABARD, 1996. Guidelines on Linking Self-Help Groups and Banks (reprinted) PRADAN, Madurai.

Remenyi, J, 1993. Where Credit is Due, Intermediate Technology Publications, London.

Roberts, R, and Harper, M, (eds.) 1980. Agricultural Credit Training, Vol. 5, lending through groups, FAO, Rome.

Robinson, M, 1994. Savings Mobilisation and Microenterprise Finance, the Indonesian experience, in: Otero M and Rhyne, E.

Rutherford, S, and Arora, SS, 1997. City Savers, DFID, New Delhi.

Rutherford, S, 1995. The Savings of the Poor, Improving Financial Services in Bangladesh, mimeo.

SANASA News, 1994. SANASA, Colombo.

SIDBI, 1997. Personal communication from K C Ranjani, Assistant General Manager.

Smiles, S, 1986. Self-Help, Penguin, London.

SPARC, 1995. Report on the Status of Women's access to credit, SPARC, Bombay.

Speechly, N, 1992. Co-ops that the Small Business can rely on, The Independent on Sunday.

Srinivasan, G, and Rao, DSK, 1996. Financing of Self-Help Groups by Banks, Some Issues, Working Paper 8, BIRD, Lucknow.

UNDP, 1996. Human Development Report, 1996, OUP, New York.

Village Banking, 1992. GEMINI Working paper no. 25, Bethesda.

Yaqub, 1995. Empowered to Default ? Small Enterprise Development, Vol. 6, no. 4.